FRANCESCA SPECTER is a London-based journalist and founder of the platform and podcast, Alonement. Prior to launching Alonement in 2019, Francesca was the deputy editor of Yahoo! Lifestyle. She has formerly worked as a reporter at the *Daily Express*, and her writing has appeared in the *Guardian*, the *Telegraph* and *Grazia*. She holds an M.A. degree in Magazine Journalism from City University, London, and she has been nominated for several awards for her work, including the PPA Digital Rising Star award. *Alonement* is Francesca's first book.

FRANCESCA SPECTRE is an independent journalist and author ... of the platform and podcast Abortment. Prior to launching Abortment in 2019, Francesca was the deputy editor at Good Lifestyle. She has formerly worked as a reporter at the Telegraph, and her writing has appeared in the Guardian, the Telegraph, and Grazia. She holds an M.A. degree in Magazine Journalism from City University London, and she has been nominated for several awards for her work, including the PPA Digital Rising Star awards. About Francesca's first book.

al●ne ment

How to be alone & absolutely own it

FRANCESCA SPECTER

QUERCUS

First published in Great Britain in 2021 by Quercus Editions Ltd

This paperback published in 2022 by

QUERCUS

Quercus Editions Ltd
Carmelite House
50 Victoria Embankment
London EC4Y 0DZ

An Hachette UK company

A CIP catalogue record for this book is available
from the British Library

PB ISBN 978 1 52941 262 8
Ebook ISBN 978 1 52941 263 5

10 9 8 7 6 5 4 3

Typeset by CC Book Production
Printed and bound in Great Britain by Clays Ltd, Elcograf S.p.A.

MIX
Paper from
responsible sources
FSC® C104740

Papers used by Quercus are from well-managed forests and other responsible sources.

For my family, Beverley, Ken and Andrew,
for giving me the love, support and space to thrive.

For my cheerleaders, best friends and brains-of-honour,
Rachel and Zoe, who have championed this idea
ever since that rainy Monday evening.

PREFACE

I used to be terrified of being alone.

Thankfully, solitude wasn't really on the agenda. I grew up in a loving, nuclear family. I have a close-knit group of friends. Aged 24, I thought I'd found the missing piece of the puzzle: the man I believed would one day be my husband. We described ourselves as a 'team'. We shared our social life, a Google Calendar and, on occasion, a toothbrush. When we spoke of the future, it would never be with the conditional 'if', but always the certain 'when'. 'Let me be your constant,' he urged me. 'I'm not going anywhere.' Our relationship was meant to be the long-term solution to my fear of loneliness. Except, after the initial honeymoon stage – of about 18 months – love wasn't quite enough. Our peers were moving in together, getting married and having children. With every engagement announcement on Facebook and every talk we had about the future, it became painfully apparent that our relationship wasn't built to last.

We stayed together for a further eight months because neither of us wanted to be single *and alone*, talking into the early hours as we tried to piece 'us' together like a logic puzzle. But a week-long argument (about the most polarising issue in the history of heterosexual relationships: throw cushions) spelled the beginning of the end. As we reached rock bottom – a shouting row in Zara Home, our words like vomited-up acid, the check-out staff genuinely scared – we decided to call time on our team of two.

Reader, it wasn't about the throw cushions.

That day, we went home, empty-handed, and sat at opposite ends of the sofa, the gulf between us made up of so much more than teal upholstery: spite, resentment, recrimination. We were over; any one of our fellow customers in Zara Home could have told you that. Yet, even after Throw-Cushion Gate, ending the relationship was one of the hardest things I've ever had to do.

Looking back, it's baffling that we spent so long in denial; that letting all that negativity fester between us felt preferable to the spectre of lives apart. But I've since realised our situation wasn't uncommon. It's no coincidence that, as social scientists at the University of Toronto observed, the fear of being single is an all-too-reliable indicator of whether a person will stay in a failing relationship.* Listening to my

---

* Stephanie Spielmann et al., 'Settling for less than out of fear of being single', *Journal of Personality and Social Psychology* (2013) 105 (6): 1049–1073. http://individual.utoronto.ca/sspielmann/Spielmann_et_al_inpress_JPSP.pdf

gut instinct – even in the face of all this fear – was a desperate last resort. Being alone, back then, felt like a punishment.

Alonement, the word that came to define my journey towards learning to appreciate alone time, was more like *atonement* for giving up my most co-dependent adult relationship in favour of – what exactly? I had no idea. The decision to end a relationship is, inevitably, a leap of faith – and, in my case, one I made when all other options were exhausted. Deciding to call time on what I once believed was the best thing that had ever happened to me felt like wilfully staying in a bad dream. In the wake of a break-up, you step, blindly, into the Great Unknown; having spent so much time focused on the magnitude of what you're losing that you have little capacity to imagine anything else.

In ending the relationship, I waved goodbye to the conventional life trajectory I thought would fortify me against loneliness: cohabiting, marriage, kids. I chose sleeping alone instead of being tucked inside the cradle of his arms; I chose cooking for one; I chose living alone; I chose having no one to wake up to and no one to say 'Goodnight' to. I chose myself, and it felt like insanity.

At the time, alone and lonely were inextricable concepts to me. I lived alone during a period when almost all of my closest friends were in relationships, and I felt my ex-boyfriend's absence like a hole in the chest. Time alone was a bitter pill I had to swallow – a tax bill; a dental filling – the price I had to pay for saying goodbye to the wrong version of

Happily Ever After. Yet, over time, the end of one relationship made way for another which was greater still: a relationship with myself.

If I could go back in time, I'd tell myself this. First of all, congratulations for making a bold decision to change your life for the better. I can't fast-forward your pain, but I'm excited for your bright future, even if you can't be. There is someone with strong, capable arms waiting for you on the other side, and that someone is *you*.

This is how alonement came to be my happy ending.

CONTENTS

INTRODUCTION

Your relationship with yourself is, by default, the most important one you will ever have. Like it or not, you entered into a non-negotiable, lifelong commitment to yourself in the hospital delivery room. Unlike any other relationship you have throughout your life, there is no room for manoeuvre. No moving out or trial separation. No 'taking it slow' or accepting you've grown apart. Family, friends and romantic partners may come and go, but your monogamous partnership with yourself is the only constant, unalterable relationship status you'll ever have.

I know! Deep breaths.

The opposite is true of our relationships with other people – the ones we spend our whole lives forming, refining and fighting for. These are inextricably connected with the certainty of loss. Statistically, half your existing friendships have a seven-year sell-by date.* Around 39 per cent of co-habiting couples break up.† Almost half of all marriages end in divorce. Even if you have the best of romantic relationships – the most rose-tinted of pairings, the 'we've been together for 70 years and now we finish each other's—' '—sentences' type – then I hate to break it to you, but (more deep breaths) 100 per cent of people die. I don't say any of this to scare you, but to help you realise that, for better and for worse, for richer and for poorer, you and, well, *you*, are in it for the long haul.

Relationship status: Alone

You are a single-person household within your own mind. This isn't a radical thing to say. We're all capable of day-dreaming about the person sitting opposite us on the train without them ever knowing about it, or spending the bulk of an hour-long meeting thinking about what we want to eat for lunch. We have a perpetual choice to stay inside our own minds, or to engage with the world around us. What *is* radical is to actually acknowledge this essential 'aloneness' – that we

---

* NWO, 'Half of Your Friends Lost in Seven Years, Social Network Study Finds', *Science Daily*, 27 May 2009. https://www.sciencedaily.com/releases/2009/05/090527111907.htm

† Harry Benson and Steve McKay, 'Commit or Quit: Living Together Longer?', *Marriage Foundation*, May 2020. https://marriagefoundation.org.uk/wp-content/uploads/2020/05/NEW-STUDY-Living-Together-Longer-Commit-or-Quit-Marriage-Week-May-2020.pdf

all live, first and foremost, inside our own heads – because we typically invest a lot of time in trying to escape this home ownership, throwing out the mortgage agreement and losing the keys.

Think about how you spend an average day. All those hours making small talk with your colleagues; WhatsApping your friends; swiping on dating apps; chatting to your mum on the phone; sweet-talking your Springer Spaniel; soothing your toddler; deciding what to have for dinner with your partner; calling British Gas (don't let the bastards get you down); replying to your boss's email out of hours; keeping up with the godforsaken Kardashians; falling asleep to an audiobook. Sound familiar? Trust me, you're not the only one avoiding your own thoughts.

As a society, we are regularly coming up with ingenious solutions to stop us looking inwards. In one well-known study conducted by Timothy Wilson, a social psychologist at the University of Virginia, a group of participants were given the option of sitting alone with their own thoughts for 15 minutes or administering themselves an electric shock. The majority went for the latter option.* But that's OK, you reason. People need people. We're social animals. It's about being connected. Nobody wants to be lonely. It's *natural*.

---

* Nadia Whitehead, 'People would rather be electrically shocked than left alone with their thoughts', *Science*, 3 July 2014. https://www.sciencemag.org/news/2014/07/people-would-rather-be-electrically-shocked-left-alone-their-thoughts

That might all be true – yet how natural is it to be so scared of being left in a room with your own thoughts that you'll electrocute yourself, just for a distraction?

As a baby, introspection comes naturally. You are born at the centre of your own universe and, even in the presence of others, you are naturally in tune with yourself. You cry when you're hungry, tired or cold. You stare in awe at a ceiling fan for twenty minutes or laugh unrestrainedly at your dad's peekaboo. The world is laid before you, and you see it from your own saucer-eyed point of view, never stopping to second-guess your reactions, or getting distracted by the presence of someone else. You begin life intimately acquainted with your wants, needs and curiosities. Around the age of two or three, you become aware of how other people see you – and modify accordingly (i.e. a bit less throwing food and randomly getting naked in supermarkets). It's not that you entirely lose your ability to behave in an instinctive way or to feel that all-encompassing sense of reverie; it's just you'll probably only act that way when no one else is around; when you're alone.

Trouble is, from here on, opportunities to fly solo are pretty scarce. You follow an accepted pattern of life whereby you spend the bulk of it searching for meaningful connections with other people – from the family home to the playground to the nightclub to the workplace to the altar to the family home (again) to the old people's home to the graveyard.

You begin your life as part of a family unit. A good

childhood is considered to be a socially connected one where your parents are around a lot and you ideally have at least one sibling, for fear of being a much-pitied only child (despite the fact that the 'only child syndrome' myth has been disproved time and time again).* You start school, where it's expected that you will play with other children in the playground and develop social skills. Speaking up in class, working well in a group and excelling at team sports are all seen as key markers of achievement as you move through the school system. University begins with Freshers' Week: a whole week (pandemic permitting) devoted not to academia but to meeting others at an accelerated pace, in drunken, sometimes regrettable set-ups. This continues into working life: open-plan offices; a constant stream of Slack messages; 'morale-boosting' mass emails from Kelly in HR; company meetings; presentations; networking evenings; Friday Happy Hour with your colleagues.

Around this time, your parents take a keen interest in whether you've 'met someone', and once you hit your late twenties being romantically unattached is regarded as a problem to be solved. *How's dating going? Are you on any apps?* Your coupled-up friends become well-meaning co-conspirators (*I have a single friend . . .*). And then – praise be! – you enter into a relationship, with the standard tick-box milestones of cohabitation, lifelong commitment

---

* 'Only child syndrome: Proven reality or long-standing myth', *Healthline*, 23 October 2019. https://www.healthline.com/health/parenting/only-child-syndrome

and eventually creating another human or two together. Any indication that you're spending time apart – holidaying separately or not moving in together quickly enough – is considered to be a warning sign. From this point onwards, your greatest social approval comes in the form of a 'she said yes!' announcement, a confetti-dotted wedding snap or a baby bump reveal.

You start a family. You grow old together. But, as you become a partner, a wife, a husband, a parent and eventually a grandparent – throughout your life – you are defined by what you are to other people. At what point, during all of this, do you get back in touch with yourself?

Alone: Heaven or hell?

Today, we're more surrounded than ever by other people's voices. There are, God help us, over a million podcasts on the App Store, Twitter has 330 million monthly active users and you can download just about any book from the Great Kindle Library In The Sky. Should you wish to, you can avoid ever being 'alone' with your thoughts – save, perhaps, in the shower (and even then, there are waterproof Bluetooth speakers). And yet, despite all those other voices doing their utmost to distract you, the inconvenient reality remains: your #nofilter inner voice can never truly be drowned out (something I'll discuss more in Chapter 2).

It's intriguing that so many of us run away from the opportunity to intimately know ourselves by opting out of our own company. We might like to hear the candid, confessional, no-holds-barred voices of *others* – exemplified by the huge sales of Tara Westover's *Educated* and Michelle Obama's *Becoming*, books centred around inspirational people who have gone on a journey of self-knowledge – yet we regularly pass up the unique opportunity we all have to get to know ourselves. That's a pretty strange decision, if you think about it; like having an access-all-areas, backstage pass to Glastonbury and choosing, instead, to stay among the screaming, beer-swilling, moshing masses.

In his 1956 book *The Art of Loving*, psychologist Erich Fromm claims that we all occupy a 'prison of aloneness': the terrifying reality that, yup, you're on your own, pal, and there is no escaping it. It's not like Fromm was against this state of aloneness. He was actually fairly pro, claiming that 'the ability to be alone is the condition for the ability to love' (more on this later, in Chapter 10). But he considered the drive to escape 'aloneness' the most essential part of the human experience. He writes: 'The deepest need of man, then, is the need to overcome his separateness, to leave the prison of his aloneness.' Adding later: 'Man – of all ages and cultures – is confronted with the solution of one and the same question: the question of how to overcome separateness, how to achieve union, how to transcend one's own individual life and find atonement.'

Were Fromm still alive today, I'd have good news and

bad news for him. The good news is, we have, as a society, come up with the best solution yet to this so-called prison of aloneness: the smartphone. I mean, you can imagine the conversation. *Hey, Erich, you know that mildly invasive landline phone that occasionally interrupts your workflow? You're going to need to sit down for this one . . .* I imagine Fromm would likely have revisited his views, had he been around to witness the invention of broadband in 1992, or the first 3G-enabled smartphone – from the Japanese company NTT DoCoMo – in 2001. Aloneness, he might have written, has become more like a drop-in centre than a prison. The bad news – not just for Fromm, but for all of us? The internet may have thrown open the gate and wedged a doorstop in front of our proverbial prison cells, but as a result we attribute little value to being alone. It's as if we got so excited during the jailbreak process that we forgot to consider what we were leaving behind.

The 'ability to be alone' – that quality Fromm considered so inherently necessary to love another person – has become a lost art. We've become socially conditioned to see our phones as the solution to every challenging thought. Feeling anxious about your 10am meeting? Scroll Instagram. Putting off the gym? Text a friend. Don't know whether to have boiled or scrambled eggs? Make a poll on Twitter! We're able to avoid the reality of aloneness at the touch of a button, and returning to it feels, more than ever, like a prison cell. But what if we could make it a haven instead? What if we could, against all odds, learn to celebrate and relax into our aloneness, to recline into it; to exhale and feel safe, inspired; without shame or embarrassment or guilt?

Alonement is the story you tell yourself

There are consolations to your essential aloneness:

- As much as alone might feel like a scary word, it also means unique. You are alone in being you.
- To acknowledge aloneness is to embrace the gift of your uniqueness, your freedom, your capacity for self-knowledge.
- Alone is when you are at your most authentic. You reconnect with that primal ability I mentioned earlier: to respond to your needs, desires and curiosities.
- It may seem isolating that you are the only person capable of hearing the voice in your head, but look at it another way. Isn't it mind-blowing that you can intimately know yourself in a way that you can never know another person – that you can read your own mind?
- Being alone means the freedom to act as an individual, not part of a pack.

When we avoid time alone, we fail to discover and capitalise on our superpowers. The change begins once you tell yourself a different story about your aloneness, and about what being alone represents. We all know that solitude can go one of two ways. Either it's a positive experience: pleasurable, comfortable and associated with a longer-term sense of fulfilment. Or (as we're socially conditioned to assume) it's a lonely, excruciating experience to be endured rather than sought out. James R. Averill, a professor of psychology at the University of Massachusetts, has concluded that an individual's ability to enjoy solitude is based on the narrative they construct around that time.* Generally, we want these stories to involve a sense of choice. Averill writes: 'What tips the balance between positive experiences of solitude and immoderate loneliness? This question can be answered in one word: *Choice*. What we call *authentic solitude* is typically based on a decision to be alone; in contrast, *pseudo solitude*, in which loneliness predominates, involves a sense of abandonment or unwanted isolation.'

It's exactly the reason why spending a sunny bank holiday relaxing in your garden might feel like bliss if you've made a proactive decision to give yourself some downtime; or hell, if you start second-guessing your lack of barbecue invitation (don't Sanjay and Grace normally organise something for this

---

* James R. Averill and Louise Sundararajan, 'Experiences of solitude: Issues of assessment, theory, and culture'. http://indigenouspsych.org/Discussion/forum/Solitude%20final.pdf

bank holiday Monday?) and spend your day trawling Instagram for evidence of your dwindling social status. 'Behind every choice is a story,' Averill writes. To choose to spend time alone – for an hour, for a day, for a week – based on the benefits you think it might bring to you is a valuable step in enjoying alonement.

The author and founder of the School of Life, Alain de Botton, introduced a similar idea on my podcast, Alonement, which I launched in March 2020. Alain was the first of a brilliant line-up of thinkers, authors and media personalities I've interviewed about their own alonement. He said: 'If we're looking for how to cure or solve the problem of loneliness, what we have to start with is changing what being on your own means. In a way, at times, all of us can feel quite comfortable being on our own, but other times it's anguishing.' So, how do you change the narrative?

Saying yes to time alone

Ostensibly, there is a straightforward solution to learning how to be alone, and that's simply (drum roll) spending time alone. Psychologist Carl Jung called the state of being alone 'the animation of the psychic atmosphere',* because it's

---

* 'The value of isolation, loneliness and solitude', *Jungian Center for the Spiritual Sciences.* https://jungiancenter.org/the-value-of-isolation-loneliness-and-solitude

where our physical solitude reflects our internal aloneness: alone in body, alone in mind. This can be an invaluable time for self-discovery. We're at one with ourselves, and our surroundings. We acknowledge and process our feelings. Our inner voices become amplified. Our ideas are most authentic. Our imaginations wander.

. . . in theory, that is.

These days, most of us aren't very good at spending time alone, so it has the potential to end up being a bit of a shitshow, not to mention the perfect breeding ground for loneliness, unhealthy habits or addictive behaviours. It's no wonder that we fear what Michael Harris, the author of *Solitude*, calls 'the bogeyman of our naked self'. For most of us, learning to be alone isn't as simple as subjecting ourselves to isolation – first, we have to tackle the scary task of coming to terms with who we actually are, which is vital groundwork for alonement.

If you think this isn't for you, I get it. I spent the best part of three decades avoiding the bogeyman, thinking silence, introspection and solitude simply weren't compatible with who I was and how I lived. Escaping aloneness felt easy and normal; facing up to it felt immeasurably harder. But just because something's easy and normalised doesn't mean it's right for you, or that you won't have to pay for it further down the line (after all, life's a long song, as my father's fond of saying). I understand all too well the discomfort that comes with facing up to your aloneness. I still feel that discomfort every single day, but, to a greater extent, I feel so many more things: strength, clarity, curiosity and a deep-seated sense of calm. Spending time alone may be your greatest fear now – as it was for me – but it could also prove your profoundest source of power. As this book explores, in a world full of ways to escape ever being alone, you will set yourself apart by embracing it. However, the answer is not simply being alone. It is alonement.

Alonement: What is it?

Alonement is a word I coined in 2019 to fill a gap in the English language (I'll take that money via bank transfer, Oxford English Dictionary). Broken down, it means 'the state of being alone' – a state we should raise up and celebrate. Reverse the syllables, and you think about alone time as an intention: 'meant to be alone'. The way I define it, alonement is quality time spent alone; it is to value and respect the time you spend with yourself. It means to be alone and absolutely own it.

The closest term, someone might butt in and suggest, is solitude; but even solitude (which, FYI, has its roots in Old French and Latin terms for 'loneliness') has an ambiguity to it: you have to qualify whether an experience is 'positive solitude', whereas alonement is, crucially, an inherently positive and valuable experience. Alonement is the direct opposite of loneliness. Think of it as a spectrum:

Loneliness < Alone > Alonement

As a dictionary entry, it would look a bit like this:

Alonement

noun

1. Quality time spent alone. *I had some really good alonement this weekend.*
2. The experience of joy and/or fulfilment when you are by yourself. *Alonement for me is a brisk walk first thing in the morning.*
3. Pleasurable solitude; also (of a solo experience) associated with a positive feeling. *It's been a hectic few months; I need an alonement holiday.*
4. The value of cherishing the time you spend alone. *Alonement is important for me and my boyfriend.*

Without the word 'alonement', I struggled to speak about being alone in a way that reflected how I felt about it. While 'alone' is ostensibly a neutral word, saying 'I feel alone' is tinged with negativity. We've all seen the Insta-cliché doing the rounds, 'Alone doesn't mean lonely'; but, for me, it never went far enough. If alone doesn't have to mean the same thing as lonely – what's the alternative? When alone is good, what is it called? Enter: alonement.

Most people *get* what alonement – which is to say they can usually think of one time in their daily routine where alone time is pretty damn good, whether that's the hot shower they take first thing or the satisfying ritual of chopping up peppers for dinner. Yet the importance of having an actual word to describe the positive feelings that being alone can generate cannot be understated. It's like Ludwig Wittgenstein said: 'The limits of my language mean the limits of my world'. If you don't have the word to describe something, it's hard to give it value and validity. You can't be what you can't see, and you can't practise what you can't define.

New words bring to life phenomena that we may have long observed but never had the language to describe. This isn't only the case for positive, empowering words; take, for instance, 'gaslighting' – in my view, one of the most import- ant contributions to the conversation about abuse and control in relationships. Gaslighting is a form of psycho- logical abuse where one partner attempts to make another question their own memory, perception and judgement, typically through denial or misinformation. The term first originated in Patrick Hamilton's 1938 play *Gas Light*, about a woman whose husband manipulates her into thinking she's going insane. It became part of psychological literature in the 1990s and has entered popular parlance over the last few years – most notably during an uproar when a recent *Love Island* contestant was accused by the charity Women's Aid of gaslighting two of the women on the show, prompting a heated national debate and a slew of articles and op-eds. Clearly, simply having a word for something can begin a cultural shift.

Alonement is my contribution to the English lexicon because I see it as embodying a necessary change in the way we acknowledge and value alone time. I've since trademarked it, and hope to one day get it into the dictionary. (If 'chirpse', 'awesomesauce' and 'promposal' all became dictionary-official last year, I like to think this isn't an impossible goal.) Occasionally you'll get someone who says you 'can't just make up words'. Of course you can (once again, see the surprisingly versatile 'chirpse'); that's literally how language was created. It's designed to serve us, and we use it to navigate the vast and ever-evolving human experience. For instance, there are many words in other languages that we don't have in English, like the Greek *meraki*, 'to do something with soul, creativity, or love; when you leave a piece of yourself in your work'. Language is power, and having a word for something previously unidentified can unlock a little part of you, or your experience, that you never quite acknowledged. Alonement, in no uncertain terms, changed my life – and I have a sneaking suspicion it might change yours, too.

Incidentally, I really, really like identifying new language to describe the 'alonement' experience. Along that principle, sprinkled throughout this book will be other terms I've adopted to help navigate our relationship with being alone, which I've listed in a glossary at the back. Among these, there's 'rubbernecking' – a term to define turning one's head to gaze at something we shouldn't, usually associated with drivers slowing down to look at car accidents.* I find it an apt term to describe our tendency to look at the lives of other people when we should be focusing on our own lives, instead – like scrolling someone else's night out on Instagram during your summer holiday. There's also Only Me-ism – a term I invented to describe our tendency to deprive ourselves of basic comforts and considerations (a fresh cafetiere, a home-cooked meal) if it's 'only me' – even though we should be our own priority.

Why me?

Learning to spend time alone isn't always easy. Take it from me: as a writer, I have one of the most solitary professions possible. I also wrote a book on being alone. While living alone. As a single person. During a pandemic.

Before my life became a giant social experiment of my own making, I was a highly sociable person: I used to love the regular Happy Hours that came with a busy office environment. Plonk me down at a first date or a large glitzy party where I know no one, and I'll be absolutely fine. 'If you're

---

* https://dictionary.cambridge.org/dictionary/english/rubbernecking

such an extrovert, why did you decide to start a platform about spending time alone?' asked comedian John Robins on an episode of my Alonement podcast. He had a point. The truth is, I started writing and podcasting about alonement because I didn't want people to fall into the same trap I had. Up until the age of 27, I was too afraid to even contemplate time alone. For most of my life, I had pursued meaningful human company above all else, while alone time held next to no value for me.

Learning to spend time alone began as a challenge to myself, which took the form of a New Year's resolution: 'learn to be alone and enjoy it'. Initially, it went against everything I had ever believed in or valued – like the thirty-six hours I once spent following the Paleo diet. It felt as natural as writing with my left hand. I'd consciously avoid making plans on a Sunday and then panic about that empty window of time as the weekend grew closer. I'd book an Odeon ticket for one, then frantically Google whether it was refundable. Meanwhile, well-meaning friends and family grew worried, assuming my uncharacteristic Greta Garbo act was simply the bravado of someone who, newly single, lacked people to hang out with when I wanted company (luckily, this was rarely the case – despite losing some couple friends in the 'divorce'). But I persisted with my resolution, despite everything (and everyone) telling me not to, and it transformed my life. Think of me, if you like, as a recovering social addict – someone who went so far towards one extreme, in my complete avoidance of alone time, that I can now speak with authority on what happens when it's lacking. I hope to convince anyone reading that if I – someone who couldn't spend so much as an hour alone – can learn to enjoy my own company, then you can too.

Others who have written about being alone include Sara Maitland, who wrote the fantastic *How To Be Alone*. She lives in a remote, rural part of Scotland and purposefully distances herself from the likes of smartphones and television. There's also Alice Koller, who wrote *The Stations of Solitude* while living alone in Nantucket Island during the dead of winter, and Henry Thoreau, who decamped to the woods for two years to write *Walden*. Do these writers have interesting backstories? Sure. Do they know a lot about solitude? No doubt, and Maitland's book in particular has proved important source material for my own. But how many of us can realistically drop everything to go and live in the woods? I know I can't. This is where alonement comes in – it's something we can all benefit from and integrate into our existing lifestyles, whatever they are. I'm telling you now because I wish I'd been able to hear it from someone who was up to their neck in a busy, socially connected city existence, rather than living a lifestyle I couldn't really relate to and didn't want to emulate.

I hope you can be inspired by my experience to go on to create your own alonement. I'm not someone who has always instinctively spent time alone, nor do I intend to spend long periods of time alone without the mitigating influence of another person. I still consider myself an extrovert who regularly 'powers up' through other people – my close friends and family are among the primary blessings of my life. But, despite all this, my eyes have been opened to the very real consequences of a fear of being alone, and I can't go back.

Alonement is about moderation

We don't really 'do' moderation in British culture. We're weekend warriors; we're crash dieters; we're intermittent fasters; we're 'work hard, play hard'. Media representations of being alone are typically extreme. We read about national loneliness epidemics, people getting married to themselves, and during the coronavirus lockdown, there was a particular appetite for stories of solo mountain climbers and around-the-world sailors and island hermits. Headline-grabbing, yes. Relatable? Not so much.

Looking to history for solitary icons, you might think of artists or composers, like Mozart, Kafka and Wordsworth. Through romanticising the reclusive genius – obsessive, cut off from society and almost exclusively white and male – and imagining theirs as the only way to be alone, we're left with something that's completely removed from our everyday lives. How could we ever emulate this intense behaviour?

Would we even want to? To be honest, just the word 'solitude' has a loftiness that I kind of resent. That's where learning to appreciate alonement comes in: quality time alone, often for short lengths of time, like a quiet afternoon or a languid weekend.

While for a select few, being alone for an extended period of time might be a failsafe recipe for an epiphany (see Taylor Swift and other geniuses – yes, the *folklore* album is a work of genius – who created masterpieces during lockdown), for others this might not work out so well. I was certainly challenged by the long stretch of alone time while living alone during the first coronavirus lockdown – four months without a hug is tough – even though I spent it writing a book about spending time alone. Did I mention I was essentially living in a social experiment of my own making?

'Just eat a balanced diet' is possibly the least marketable weight loss advice, but long term it's the most rewarding, and this analogy equally applies to spending time alone. According to Michael Harris: 'Solitude and connection are elements in a larger social diet. We need both – just like we need carbohydrates and fats – but we can do damage to ourselves by consuming too much of either.' Rather than undertaking long periods of solitude, most of us benefit from a balance of regular moments of retreat from others. Social connection and alone time require a delicate balancing act, and alonement is a word that acknowledges the importance of both.

As I mentioned earlier, simply being alone is rarely a magic bullet for any sort of self-growth. We all know – some more than others – how alone time can devolve into our most destructive tendencies and addictive behaviours, including everything from obsessively checking social media and the news to eating and exercise disorders, drugs and alcohol dependency. Or else, alone time can be spent in a sort of relatively harmless, hedonistic way: binge-watching box sets, mindlessly snacking, idly scrolling Instagram. You might be alone – but you sure as hell won't be reaping any benefits typically associated with solitude. Alonement means thinking proactively about how you can turn this time into a positive experience.

It's about quality – not quantity. By focusing on alonement as a value used to inform your day-to-day life, you'll find it easier to settle on a version that works for your situation. Because, while alonement *can* be a solo trip to another country, it's more often the ten minutes before work you spend making coffee and sitting down to savour it, or the hour of phone-free time you give yourself before bed to journal or rearrange your sock drawer or simply stare into space. Taking this time may not seem like a particularly big deal, and you may question whether it's enough to really impact your life. Bear with me. One thing you can be certain of with alonement is that you get back more than you put in. Try making a little space for it in your life, and you'll begin to see just how powerful it can be.

What counts as 'alone'?

As I write this, sitting by myself in a one-bed flat, I am alone in perhaps the most obvious way. My phone is on Airplane mode, the radio is off and – given that I live by myself – I'd be shocked if someone else walked in through the front door. The only way I could be more 'alone' is if you were to relocate this set-up to the Outer Hebrides. Or maybe Mars. Yet, this is far from the only way to be alone. I consider alonement to be in action when I write in the café down the road. On holiday with friends, I seek out alonement by going for a walk alone on the beach, or swimming far out into the sea and looking out into the horizon. When I worked in an open-plan office, alonement was disappearing off to a different floor and hiding in a booth, or else it was wearing noise-cancelling headphones at my desk. Sometimes alonement is when I let my mind wander, the way I used to get lost in my imagination during maths lessons. Alonement is, actually, all around (that sounds even better if you imagine Hugh Grant saying it) – and I'm going to show you how to find it and get the most from it.

The multi-textured joy of being alone

Alonement isn't just about having a good time. Don't get me wrong – it totally lends itself to joy. As you become more and more comfortable with the idea of spending time alone, alonement *can* simply be a comfy night in watching *Friends* in your flannel pyjamas, with fish and chips and a glass of rosé (now there's a plan, I'll be doing exactly that later on). That's the kind of evening that can be all sorts of fun whether or not anyone else is there. Plus, there's often a deliciousness inherent in choosing *exactly* what you want to do, right down to the precise volume of the television. That said, alonement offers another type of satisfaction; a more meaningful, life-affirming type of pleasure.

Aristotle termed this 'eudaimonic' happiness: a loftier sort of satisfaction derived from living with meaning and purpose. Your pyjama-clad night in watching *Friends* looks more like what the ancient Greeks called 'hedonic' pleasure: a more straightforward, fleeting pleasure-based kind of happiness. Basically, alonement is when time alone is positive, and this might be because it's enjoyable, or because it's valuable, but it doesn't necessarily have to be both. Sure, you *can* experience hedonic pleasure as a person alone, and often that happens in a much purer and authentically 'you' way than it might with another person: tucking into a meal *you* love, dancing like no one's watching (because no one's watching).

But other times alonement serves as a space of regeneration and self-growth: writing in a journal, or going to bed early rather than staying up *again* to binge-watch Netflix with your housemates. Both are worth practising, for different reasons.

When it comes to hedonic pleasure, it's crucial for us to acknowledge to ourselves (and indeed to others) that it is valid to do things alone purely for your own pleasure (and I don't just mean a night in with your vibrator). As an extrovert, I used to draw almost all of my hedonic pleasures from being around other people, where there's a momentum and an energy which is harder to find in solitude. Yet, it is still possible with the right planning to have a fun (and in no way highbrow) evening alone. Some of my happiest times have been spent reading fiction or watching trashy TV. That said, while fleeting pleasures are all well and good, alonement is fertile ground for finding meaning and purpose in your life. As I'll discuss in Chapter 5, spending time alone is not only a key ingredient for productivity and creativity, it's also a space where you can reflect on where that meaning and purpose lies.

Who is this book for?

For me, living alone as a single person – latterly, during a pandemic – has been an incubation state for getting to know myself very well. But this is by no means a book aimed solely at 'single' people or those who live alone. Whether you're single, in a relationship, married, or 'not putting a label on things' with Greg, 34, from Plenty of Fish, your relationship with yourself is the only one guaranteed to be lifelong.

Certainly, being single, divorced or widowed can present opportunities for working out who you are as an individual, in a similar way to how other major life changes – career shifts, moving house, parenthood, a worldwide pandemic – force us to re-evaluate who we are. That said, having been in multiple serious relationships, I've established that being one half of a couple in no way immunises you from loneliness or suppresses a need for self-knowledge; in fact, it's all too often the opposite.

Learning to thrive alone – whether that's travelling solo or simply learning to relish the nights your partner or flat-mate is away from home – is something we can all work on. Being alone is how we come into the world and how we die; we will all at some point in our lives be alone. Of course, there are times when we lean on kindness from others, and interpersonal relationships will play a huge part in our lives. But alonement will fortify you in a deeper way than your relationships with others ever can.

This book is for anyone who struggles to spend time alone.

This book is for anyone who is naturally good at spending time alone but worries deep down that it's a bad thing.

This book is for those worried they will never meet 'The One'.

This book is for those who *have* met 'The One' and wonder why they still don't feel happy with their lives.

This book is for those whose friends have all coupled up and they're sick with envy, secretly hoping a right-swipe on Tinder could make all the building blocks of their life fall into place.

This book is for couples who struggle to maintain their independence.

This book is for anyone who's ever struggled with their identity outside of their friends, family or wider community.

This book is for anyone who avoids pursuing their passions, because they can't find someone to take along with them.

This book is for everyone in a relationship with themselves.

This book is for, well, everyone.

How this book works

It's almost time for you to go forth and conquer your alone time; but first, a little about how I put this book together. I'm well aware – as someone who never 'got' alone time – why you might need a little convincing, so when writing this book, it felt important to balance the 'why' and the 'how' of being alone. I wanted to give a bit of theory to debunk the way we, as a society, see alone time and shift the stigma, but also to provide plenty of practical tips for actually making alonement happen. As I've already mentioned, alonement isn't just being by yourself – it's proactive quality time that requires work, just like any relationship – so I've packed each chapter full of ways to harness your alonement and make it work for you. From self-care to making time for your passions and physically carving out your own space wherever you are, I want to show you how to make the world your alonement oyster.

As for actually reading the book, I'd advise starting at the beginning (groundbreaking, I know) and reading the first two chapters before you skip ahead to anything else, as they are essential for understanding the concept of alonement. Ideally, from there, you'll just keep on reading as nature (I'm nature, in this instance) intended. But if you're looking for specific advice – say you've got an upcoming solo holiday or are feeling the need for some breathing space in your relationship – feel free to jump ahead to the relevant chapter (that's Chapter 7 and Chapter 10 in those cases).

A quick disclaimer: I want to stress that this book won't change your life by itself. Yes, you did read that correctly. Think of this initial investment simply as a leaping-off point – because the work goes beyond your bookshelf. You don't just follow @dailyselfgrowth104 on Instagram in January and, hey presto, you're a self-actualised human having scrolled through 23 post updates. It doesn't work like that. The only way you can discover the value of time alone is experiencing it first hand yourself, by integrating it in both little and large ways into your regular routine. There may be some discomfort and doubt along the way, but I guarantee that it will snowball into something that is truly life-affirming. Once you understand the value of alonement, it's self-sustaining and will stay with you your whole life. Your practice will ebb and flow (in the face of relationships and work pressures, for instance) but you will regularly feel the pull to return to yourself, like a beloved friend, and make that time and space for alonement. As I say, this book won't change your life. But you can.

Lastly, whatever you do, I suggest you read this book when you're alone: phone in a drawer and/or on mute, partner or housemate also on mute (or at least politely requested to respect your reading time) and your full attention. No social media (plenty of time to post the cover on the grid later). For now, this is your time.

Welcome to alonement.

1

WHY WE NEED ALONEMENT

For most of my life, I was my least favourite person to spend time with. OK, I'd have drawn the line at a candlelit dinner with, say, Josef Fritzl, but looking back, I am amazed at the lengths I went to just to avoid alone time. I'd jump at any opportunity to socialise. A last-minute invite to a bar in the furthest part of Peckham? I'd be straight on that bus – all 75 minutes of it. A friend of a friend's cousin was hosting a barbecue, and asked if I wanted to join? Why not! If a Tinder date suggested meeting up on a work night in mid-November, I'd be like, yeah, sure, I love Wetherspoons – 9pm sounds *perfect*.

Overcommitted, overstretched and overspent; my *raison d'être*, it seemed, was to get as far away from myself as I could. It wasn't self-loathing as much as a deeply held belief that being around other people was what gave my life meaning.

Time alone was just a drab waiting room to tolerate until real life resumed; it held so little value to me. Solitude was a chore, something I was lumbered with doing enough of already. That's why, when deliberating between spending a night by myself or pursuing pretty much any other option, I'd so often pick the latter.

Up until the age of 27, I had always lived with other people: family, flatmates, partners. I struggled with a couple of living arrangements where I lived with just one other person – meaning I would be alone some of the time. Rather than relishing the nights my flatmate was out to have a bit of 'me-time', I'd check our shared wall calendar and try to make plans so I was out, too. When being physically around people wasn't possible, I'd connect with others virtually – firing off dozens of messages into a WhatsApp group or sharing my life in an Instagram Story. I couldn't even watch a film alone without messaging throughout.

I spoke to author and journalist Poorna Bell about this in an episode of my Alonement podcast. Poorna discovered her love of alonement in her thirties and, before then, she – like me – had never stopped to consciously schedule 'alone time'. 'Thinking about being alone or actively carving out time to be alone is something I don't think I was even aware of [when I was younger]. In a way, you go from your family home to being at school to uni, where you're with people all the time, and you go from uni to flat shares. I don't think that I ever really gave it much thought. I didn't actively say, *do I need to do XYZ, do I need to make sure that I've got time for myself on the weekend?* I would just react to whatever was going on and whoever would invite me out.'

Learning to value alone time is, without a doubt, the most radical and important lesson I've learnt in my life to date. So, what was it that stopped me from spending any time alone for the best part of three decades? I think it came down to three factors:

1. The fact that we live in a society where being sociable is disproportionately rewarded
2. A deep, despairing fear of time alone and all it stands for
3. Being digitally connected 24/7, courtesy of a multi-billion-dollar tech industry that feeds on this primal fear of being alone like it's catnip

Sound familiar?

Society smiles on the extrovert

Let's start with reason number 1. I honestly used to think avoiding alone time was simply part of who I was. I firmed up this conviction after doing a personality test at school, which told me I am an 'extrovert'. That seemed to make sense: I made friends easily and I was good at parties. This was all socially applauded behaviour, and no one ever told me that my attitude was unhealthy. My mother – a natural introvert – was the only person who questioned my jam-packed social life: 'What about your time for *you*?' I'd sigh inwardly, thinking, *I'm an extrovert. I don't need alone time, Mum.*

For the uninitiated, the broad definition of an extrovert is someone who is more outgoing and sociable, compared with their shyer, more reserved counterparts. Think of it like a battery. While an introvert's energy levels are charged up by spending time alone, extroverts are the opposite and time spent with others gets us all fired up and raring to go. We're the people talking to fill the gaps in conversation; FaceTiming you out of the blue; organising social gatherings and work drinks. We give gushing, rapid-fire responses to texts; we're the life and soul of the party; we wear our hearts on our sleeves. We're bounding, brown-eyed Labradors to your Siamese cat. The Tigger to your Eeyore. The Lorelai to your Rory.

The extrovert versus introvert theory is used to inform almost all popular personality tests, including the Myers–Briggs Type Indicator. Between half and 74 per cent of the population fall into the 'extrovert' category, depending on which study you believe. Some are more sceptical about labelling people as either/or, and with good reason. Nowadays, a great number of people I speak to will acknowledge a grey area: 'I'm an extrovert who likes spending time alone', 'I'm a secret introvert' or 'I'm an extrovert but I'm really shy'. I see the value in these qualifications. Still, the extrovert/introvert distinction remains an important one and, broadly speaking, we identify with one or the other in terms of how we energise ourselves. No matter how much I have learnt to value alone time, I remain puffed up with energy after a night chatting with strangers at a Soho pub.

There's no definitive answer for what makes us an extrovert or an introvert, but it's likely down to our genetics. So, which side won in the genetic lottery? Ostensibly, the extroverts. It's no secret that extroverted types enjoy an unfair privilege in society. Take it from me: I *am* one. Back when I worked at a US tech company where socialising was strongly encouraged, I would skip into an after-work Happy Hour with the zeal of a six-year-old in a sweet shop, while my much more introverted colleague quietly confessed to me that she was only attending 'to show willing'. Modern society is an extrovert's playground, from those first schooldays to navigating the workplace – and this is particularly the case in major cities where people compete to be the biggest and the brightest. From the meme-generating appeal of Gemma Collins to our obsession with the flamboyant Rose family on *Schitt's Creek*, as a society we're often drawn to gregarious, social types over the quieter and more aloof.

This suggests that introverts get the bum deal. In her book, *Quiet: The Power of Introverts in a World That Can't Stop Talking*, Susan Cain bemoans what she considers a cultural bias against introverts. She cites findings that the vast majority of teachers consider the ideal student to be an extrovert, who can adapt well to the high-stimulation environment of big classrooms. The same bias is true of offices, where extroverts are 25 per cent more likely to land a top job. As a result, she argues, we socially condition children towards extroversion, praising them for 'coming out of their shell'.

The extrovert is like society's favourite child. No matter what they do, no matter how many wine glasses they knock over at a party or people they accidentally offend, they will be smiled upon far more than the introvert. Meanwhile, introverts are told from childhood that their approach is 'wrong'. Be more confident! Speak up! Be less stand-offish! Open up more! While introverts are conditioned to act more like extroverts in certain environments, such as at work and at parties, extroverts are waved past with a Get Out Of Jail Free card at almost every stage of life. Except, there's a catch.

Extroverts fail at being alone

While introverts are encouraged to work against their natural instincts, extroverts are almost never encouraged to do the opposite: to learn to spend time alone. This means that an incapacity for positive solitude is never identified as a problem, or an area for self-development. And this, as I explain in this book, can have damaging effects, proving just as limiting as certain introverted behaviours.

Often, highly sociable people are so scared to be alone that they'll do almost anything to avoid it. And I mean anything. For context, here's a not-at-all comprehensive list of what I, as an extrovert, have prioritised above being alone:

- Drinking Chardonnay into the early hours of Saturday morning with colleagues I had already spent the whole week with
- Participating in a 127-message-long Messenger thread about what colour knickers we should buy a hen
- Listening to a colleague describe, in excruciating detail, her child's morning bowel movements in the office kitchen
- Staying on for a requisite second drink with a date who later sent me an unprompted list of criticisms regarding my most recently published articles
- Offering countless therapy sessions to my friends on WhatsApp
- Travelling for 80 minutes to attend a friend of a friend's birthday, where I knew no one else, just so I wouldn't be staying in on a Saturday night
- Staying up until 2am messaging someone I had only just matched with on Hinge
- Sharing the precious opening moments of a gig in an Instagram Story

It's true that being an extrovert has its perks, but behind closed doors, it can also translate into an instinctive neediness which sees you putting almost any social activity above time to yourself – as the list above will testify.

You can imagine how that works in romantic relationships. While I struggled with some aspects of having a partner, the notion of 'needing space' – something that, as I discussed with John Robins on my Alonement podcast, is actually essential for a healthy relationship (more on that in Chapters 8 and 10) – seldom crossed my mind. I'd happily latch on to my ex's social plans, if the alternative meant spending time alone. Writing a diary and reading – solitary practices I've done on and off all my life, and nowadays couldn't go a day without – were cast aside because I actively chose being with him over most other things. We did everything together – even showering (in the least erotic set-up possible, one of us brushing our teeth and the other lathering up Head & Shoulders) – because it afforded us fewer moments apart.

Being an extrovert was a good thing, I reasoned, and so was being in a relationship, so I took both those things to the extreme, treating my natural inclination to favour social interaction over time spent alone as a sort of inevitability. I thought that by being around others as much as possible, then I was giving myself what I needed, taking my 'extrovert' label to the extreme. Alone, for me, would always be lonely, because I didn't know any other way to see it. It never occurred to me that, in devoting all my time to other people,

I was missing the opportunity to get to know myself. That giving little bits of myself away to everyone meant I didn't have enough left just for me.

I was reminded of this when I interviewed author and journalist Daisy Buchanan for the podcast. Daisy is one of the most magnetic people I've ever met, yet she spoke passionately of her growing need to spend time alone. 'I do find that when I'm around people I really find it very, very hard to hold myself back. I want to be pleased around them, I want to be in a good mood for them. I think I give a lot of energy; I want to bring people up,' she said, adding, 'but the older I get, the more I find I need that time to recharge.' For Daisy, the value of time alone is to protect 'a core of me that I don't have to share'. Over the past couple of years, I've been through a similar process to Daisy, learning to moderate what I 'give' of myself socially. What's been inherent to that process is learning to overcome a deep-seated (albeit all too common) social anxiety about what being alone says about me.

The 'Saturday Night Fear'

Some of our earliest negative experiences of being alone come from our school days. While in adulthood we may have a more comprehensive understanding of places we're comfortable being alone (maybe at home, or in a coffee shop, but less so in a crowded restaurant at the weekend), as a young child the potential for highly visible social rejection is everywhere: from feeling left out in the playground to getting picked last for the rounders team (on a side note, PE teachers are sadists for perpetuating this practice). While an inability to catch a ball might not hinder you in later life, the aftershocks of social rejection do. According to a study of 5,000 subjects by Purdue University in the United States, the pains of ostracism can result in long-term feelings of alienation and depression.*

Introverts and extroverts alike are haunted by what spending time alone might say about them, and it complicates our ability to pursue self-growth through alonement. This fear often rears its ugly head during our teenage or early adult years, for instance at school or university, when playground politics are eclipsed by more complicated social dynamics. On my Alonement podcast, author and illustrator Florence Given talked about her experience as a 14-year-old at high school where she was 'ousted' from her friendship 'clique'. Rather than try and rejoin the group, she made a conscious decision to stay out of it, reasoning: 'I wasn't comfortable with the person I was becoming in this clique ... the things I would have to do to stay in it, like being loud and disruptive in class.' Showing wise-beyond-her-years levels of foresight, Florence opted to

---

* Purdue University, 'Pain of Ostracism Can Be Deep, Long-Lasting', *Science Daily*, 6 June 2011. https://www.sciencedaily.com/releases/2011/05/110510151216. htm

'choose myself over the validation which came from being in this group'. She adds that it was 'the best decision I ever made' but also 'the hardest ever'.

Long after school, social anxiety can centre around certain 'stigma times' associated with loneliness. I discussed this on the podcast with BBC Radio London presenter Jo Good who, despite her chatty on-air persona, identifies as a 'private introvert'. Jo is happy to be alone: aged 65, she's lived by herself for the past 30 years, and loves nothing more than coming home to an empty flat. Yet, she said, she can't bear to see the New Year in by herself – 'Even I would think that was sad,' she admitted – and, annually at 11.45pm on 31 December, she finds herself heading from her flat to her local pub in Marylebone, just so she can raise a glass in the company of strangers. In another episode of the podcast, author and journalist Sophia Money-Coutts confessed similar feelings of shame around being alone at the weekend: 'It's so weird how essentially my perfect night is sitting on the sofa having a takeaway with a bottle of wine watching a box set, yet if it's a Friday or a Saturday there's something that feels inherently quite sad about that.'

These conversations reminded me of a long-held fear of my own. Growing up in London, Saturday night was the prime window of social opportunity at the weekend. As a result, I spent a decade plotting ways to never be home alone, my 17-year-old self panicking midweek if I hadn't made plans or wasn't invited to a party I knew others were going to. Recently, *Glamour* dubbed the 'Saturday Scaries'* – the fear that you don't have plans on a Saturday night – the new 'Sunday Scaries' (which centre around anxiety about the week to come). At university, every night was 'Saturday night', and the social pressure felt relentless in an environment where it seemed everyone around me was socialising, all the time. People talk about the FOMO inflicted by seeing others having fun on social media, but at least that's on an opt-in basis. There's nothing more loneliness-inducing than hearing laughter in another room, through the too-thin walls in your halls of residence, and knowing you were not invited to whatever's going on.

Amid my fruitless attempts to gain BNOC ('Big Name On Campus') status, it never occurred to me that alone time was something to consider, let alone factor in. I hadn't exactly cultivated a taste for restorative, life-affirming alonement as a teenager, and I wasn't about to do so over £1 Jägerbombs. Time spent alone was functional: for doing coursework or exercising, and often not even then – we'd flock, en masse, to the library, or chat to one another on adjacent treadmills at the gym. I spent so much time proving – to whom, I'm not quite sure – that I was capable of finding someone to spend time with. Looking back, university was undeniably the most sociable period of my life; yet I spent most of it worrying about being alone.

---

* Sara Macauley, 'Why Saturday Scaries are WAY more real than the ones we get on a Sunday', *Glamour*, 29 August 2020. https://www.glamourmagazine.co.uk/article/saturday-anxiety-is-more-than-sunday

I'm not the only one. I have close friends who have felt a similar pressure to book out their entire social calendars, or who will avoid doing activities they would enjoy alone (visiting art exhibitions, going to the cinema) simply because they hate the idea of being seen alone in public. And, because society favours extroverted behaviour, no one tells you to act any differently. Instead, they will say: 'You're so popular/sociable/busy.' My friend Hannah, 28, says: 'If I have a quiet day at the weekend without any plans, I find myself thinking: "Why am I by myself? What does this say about me to other people?"' Hannah grew up in a highly sociable family within the close-knit Jewish community of northwest London, and long believed that being alone wasn't an option: 'It wasn't normal to not have a plan on a Saturday night, or not to be seeing groups of friends at different times throughout the week.' It's only in the past couple of years she's learnt the importance of withstanding this pressure: 'As fun as it might be at the time, you come crashing down if you don't have regular time to yourself for emotional downtime.'

Post-university, my own Saturday Night Fear returned. Aged 27, when my ex-boyfriend and I broke up (and most of my friends were coupled up), I realised that one of the things I was most afraid of was if someone asked me what I'd done during the weekend, and I would have to admit I'd spent part of it – shock, horror – alone. I envisaged the coming years as an endless string of solitary nights on the sofa. At a time when I needed time alone to piece myself together again – to remember who I was without my ex – I instead channelled my energy into maniacally organising Saturday night plans, as if finding myself alone on any given weekend might be the measure of my failing to cope without my ex, not the very real (and normal) heartbreak I was working through.

Thankfully, despite my Saturday Night Fear, I've never felt short of genuine connection and friendship. My social anxiety around Saturday nights – like Hannah's – was bound up in a cultural sense of what time alone might say about me, especially in what I *perceived* as a vulnerable, stigmatised state of being single (more on this in Chapter 9). For me, the cure for this particular hang-up was twofold.

The first part was facing my fear one weekend in February 2019, soon after making my 'enjoy being alone' New Year's resolution. I'd been speaking to my cousin Sam – one of the most cultured millennials I know – about my plans for the coming weekend, and mentioned, a little embarrassed, that I was going to spend Saturday night alone (secretly hoping to make a last-minute plan). Instead, Sam reeled off a list of brilliant film recommendations and the idea of a movie night in, by myself, took shape; for the first time in my life, a Saturday night with no social plans seemed like an opportunity rather than a disaster. As I lay horizontal on my sofa under a cosy blanket that evening, credits rolling and the remnants of a Thai takeaway in front of me, I wondered what had taken me so long. In psychological terms, I administered myself some exposure treatment. On the podcast, Florence

Given spoke about doing a similar exercise when she was a teenager, when she challenged herself to lie alone in a field around other students from her school, in order to conquer one of her biggest fears at the time: 'being judged by other people and not having control over other people's perceptions'. It was a success: 'I thought if I can look like a weirdo and get through this, I can get through anything,' she said.

The second part of this cure? Acknowledging that – actually, in the nicest possible way – no one gave a flying fuck if I wasn't out on a Saturday night.

The fear of our own thoughts

Of course, it's not just a fear of being 'unpopular' that keeps us from spending time with ourselves. Often, when we avoid time alone, there's a method to the madness: it's to get away from the uncomfortable business of sitting down and thinking deeply. Whether it's booking back-to-back social engagements weeks in advance, using our partners or friends as emotional crutches or simply sharing our whole lives on social media, many of us will do whatever it takes to avoid really facing up to ourselves. 'I struggle in my own company. A lot of the time I'm not good with my own thoughts, especially if I'm not feeling 100 per cent in myself, mentally,' says Hannah. 'The thought of being alone and having the time to process things – it's not good.' Instead, she fills her time with non-stop activities: baking, seeing friends, doing puzzles. But this busy-ness (while admirable on one level) is often, she admits, a means of getting away from what might await her when she pauses.

Hannah's approach is more normal than not. So, why are we so scared of our own thoughts? When I spoke to Alain de Botton for my podcast, he (characteristically) hit the nail on the head: 'Being on your own is, for many people, not just a bit boring, it's positively frightening – it's horrible because you're in danger of stumbling upon bits of information that will require pain in one way or another. The pain of mourning, the pain of needing to take action, the pain of realising that life isn't what you want it to be.'

In short, feelings are messy, unpleasant, and we don't like to have to confront them, because not only can they be painful, but they could also necessitate a radical – and particularly inconvenient – rearranging of our lifestyles. Except, once we acknowledge this, the danger is apparent. Because if you're too scared to confront and act upon your thoughts, then you're left in a state of stagnation that might prevent you from leaving a toxic friend, abusive partner or unsuitable living situation. In this context, alone time with your thoughts is not just valuable; it's a lifeline, empowering you to change your life for the better.

The psychoanalyst Ester Schaler Buchholz, author of *The Call of Solitude: Alonetime in a World of Attachment*, was concerned by this fear of being alone. 'In contrast to attachment, people view time and solitude in greater trepidation,' she wrote back in 1995. Yet she considered time by oneself – which she termed 'alonetime' – to be 'essential to human happiness and survival' in the same way as engaging with others is. 'Without solitude existing as a safe place, a place for long sojourns and self-discovery, we lose the important sense of being self-regulating individuals.' And that's just it. If we don't have the ability to be alone, then we will always end up leaning on other people. To befriend this solitude is to gain precious autonomy over your life and bring your best self to your relationships.

I = Phone

Towards the end of the noughties we found the greatest solution yet to facing our 'aloneness': the smartphone, an all-singing, all-dancing, ever-present device that we look at, on average, once every 12 minutes (that's 95 times a day).* The majority of British people (57 per cent) admit to using their phones on the toilet† – and, after further interrogation

---

* 'A decade of digital dependency', *Ofcom*, 2 August 2018. https://www.ofcom. org.uk/about-ofcom/latest/media/media-releases/2018/decade-of-digital-dependency
† Matthew Smith, 'Most Britons use their phone on the toilet', *YouGov*, 28 February 2019. https://yougov.co.uk/topics/lifestyle/articles-reports/2019/02/28/most-britons-use-their-phone-toilet

of some friends at the pub, it appears the remaining 43 per cent are, in fact, lying.

The 'i' in 'iPhone' stands for 'internet', but nowadays our identities are so bound up with these devices that you'd be forgiven for interpreting it otherwise. It is very easy – 'normal', even – to never, ever be alone at all. 'The largest, most powerful companies that have ever existed are devoted to producing distraction machines,' Michael Harris tells me. 'In the same way as McDonalds capitalises on our appetites for food, tech companies capitalise on our desires for social connection. We've always had the capacity to be distracted from our solitude, but now we are at an overwhelming moment in history where solitude is being elbowed out of our daily lives until we have none at all. The goal, of course, is always to parcel up as much attention as possible, and sell it to advertisers,' he adds.

Every time you scroll Instagram idly on the tube, or WhatsApp your way through your lunch break, technology companies' bid for your attention has proved a shining success. Modern living is something of an enabler in avoiding alone time, because even if we're not physically alone, our smartphones – which come everywhere with us – give us the impression of being sociable 24/7, ostensibly 'connecting' us with friends at the touch of a button. We are constantly at the behest of others, and it's something we invite into our lives, our dinner tables, our workplaces. More than half of us (54 per cent) are affected by a legitimate phobia of being parted from our phones, known as 'nomophobia', which is linked to feelings of personal inadequacy and inferiority.* Is that because we might have time to pursue a challenging thought to completion before – *DING*?

While you might think a night on the sofa with your iPhone counts as being alone, experts firmly disagree. Schaler Buchholz suggests phone users (nowadays, virtually all of us) are increasingly sacrificing their solitude due to the effect of technology. Of course, Schaler Buchholz was writing back in 1995, a year which saw the release of the then-revolutionary Nokia Ringo (which had an aerial and was roughly the length and weight of a brick), but she quite eerily forecasted a time when 'portable phones, pagers and data transmission devices of every sort will keep us terminally in touch'. One can only imagine what her reaction to the almighty iPhone X, and how much it hinders our ability to value solitude, might have been.

Sherry Turkle, psychologist and author of *Alone Together: Why We Expect More from Technology and Less from Each Other*, gave a more up-to-date critique in a TED Talk in 2012. 'The moment people are alone, even for a few seconds, they become anxious, they panic, they fidget. They reach for a device,' she said. 'Being alone feels like a problem that needs to be solved, and so people try to solve it by connecting. But

---

* OnePoll, via *The Telegraph*. https://www.telegraph.co.uk/technology/news/10267574/Nomophobia-affects-majority-of-UK.html

it doesn't solve an underlying problem.' If we're reaching for our phones on average every 12 minutes of our waking life, it's no wonder that we fail to process our thoughts and feelings, believing instead that the answers to our problems are all available on our social networks, just an arm's length away. On the one hand, it's good to know you can reach out to and be there for friends instantaneously, but it means we're becoming worse and worse at processing our own emotions. This leaves us messaging our friends for the most basic decisions, when a) they might be busy, and b) surely we are the best person to take control of our situation. When we outsource so many of our problems – big and small – to others, we lose the ability to check in with ourselves in the first place. 'It's as if we're using [other people] as spare parts to support our fragile sense of self,' says Turkle. Like Schaler Buchholz before her, Turkle believes passionately in the power of solitude: 'If we're not able to be alone, we're going to be more lonely.'

But we can't just blame technology for getting in between us and solitude. It's here to stay and is simply a reflection (or intensification) of the society we live in, holding a mirror both to our broader societal values (extroversion) and our inner-most fears (being alone). Plus, on a practical level, having an iPhone can be invaluable when you're by yourself, to help you navigate a journey on Google Maps or reassure your friends you're alive during a solo trip. To pursue a healthy relation-ship with technology, we need to make it serve us – not the other way around. But first we have to acknowledge the need for (offline) alone time in the first place.

We all need alone time

What I know now is that, for introverts and extroverts alike, being alone is a necessary and improving state. You might just need the occasional Saturday night in, or you might, at the other end of the spectrum, prefer to spend most of your time alone or with people you know very well – but the requirement for at least some alonement is a universal one.

This was highlighted in a recent study* conducted by the University of California. The researchers asked a group of young students how much time they spent alone and why they chose to do it. Reasons ranged from 'I feel energised' and 'I enjoy the quiet' to 'I feel uncomfortable around others'. Those who reported 'maladaptive solitude' – i.e. for nega-tive reasons – were at greater risk of depression, whereas those who practised 'adaptive solitude' – i.e. choosing to be alone for personal growth reasons – faced none of these risks, leading the scientists to conclude time spent alone, in the right way, could 'improve wellbeing'. The most inter-esting part of the write-up, for me, was co-author Dr Virginia

---

* Jennifer McNulty, 'Teens who seek solitude may know what's best for them, research suggests', *UC Santa Cruz Newscenter*, 22 March 2019. https://news.ucsc.edu/2019/03/azmitia-solitude.html

Thomas's conclusion that solitude serves exactly the same function for introverts and extroverts; 'Introverts just need more of it.'

Alonement is also vital to proper relaxation. In 2016, 18,000 people in 134 countries completed the Rest Test – the world's biggest survey on rest.* All of the top five activities cited as 'most relaxing' were either exclusively solitary ones or linked to solitude:

- Reading (58 per cent)
- Being in the natural environment (53.1 per cent)
- Being on their own (52.1 per cent)
- Listening to music (40.6 per cent)
- Doing nothing in particular (40 per cent)

Meanwhile, sociable activities like seeing friends and family, or drinking alcohol in company, didn't even feature in the top ten. And yet how often do we consciously make this link between relaxing and being alone, or spell it out to others? Neglecting to factor alone time into your lifestyle is like forever forgetting to add the all-essential 'baking powder' to a cake recipe. We *all* need alonement – as a value in and of itself – to be our best, most authentic selves, and yet we live in an extrovert-centric, tech-obsessed world designed to

---

* Wellcome, 'Results of world's largest survey on rest to be announced', press release, 27 September 2016. https://wellcome.org/press-release/results-worlds-largest-survey-rest-be-announced

encourage anything but. I'm not a fan of conspiracy theories, but don't you think it's strange that the world conspires to keep you, and you, apart?

The fear of being alone could ruin your life

Does that sound dramatic? Good – because it should. You'll likely know a number of people whose lives appear fuelled by a fear of time alone. Do any of these scenarios ring a bell?

- The friend whose social calendar is booked up for the next six months
- That couple who *really* need to break up
- The ever-present colleague at the tea station
- The Tinder match still texting you from last week's date even though it was a mutual flop
- That Instagram user you follow who replies to DMs at breakneck speed

At the heart of it, this seemingly innocuous behaviour is symptomatic of a society where phone addiction and busyness is standard fare. The fear associated with being alone with your thoughts is one hell of a meaty subject, and – don't you worry – the next chapter is devoted to that very fear (and how to work on it). But first, I want to address how wholly damaging that 'normality' is.

As Sara Maitland writes in *How To Be Alone*: 'We have arrived at a cultural moment when we are terrified of something that we are not reliably, or healthily, able to evade. Solitude can happen to anyone; we are all at risk.' She's right to raise the alarm. The consequences of not confronting our fear of being alone are weighty, and, at some point down the line, we're likely to suffer as a result. An essay on the School of Life website* deems the fear of being alone 'one of the single greatest contributors to human misery and the driver of some of our weightiest and most unfortunate decisions'. I'm glad someone's taking it seriously. A short list of consequences might include:

- Staying in the wrong relationship
- Tolerating toxic behaviour or emotional abuse
- Having children just to keep a relationship going
- Never quite getting round to writing that novel
- Ignoring your real sexuality
- Staying friends with people you don't even like that much
- Waking up in 30 years and realising you're married to the wrong person
- Waking up in 45 years and realising you never did anything on your bucket list

---

* School of Life, 'The High Price We Pay for Our Fear of Being Alone'. https://www.theschooloflife.com/thebookoflife/the-high-price-of-the-fear-of-loneliness

I'll put it this way. We may not be able to escape being alone, but we do a bloody good job of pretending otherwise. And, long term? It's the emotional equivalent of a dental cavity.

Take it from me: after spending a lifetime avoiding being alone, I finally realised that maybe it was time to start leaning into it. If my fear of being alone had perpetuated my relationship long beyond what was healthy, it was clear it had the potential to jeopardise my life. This alone time, while daunting, was a gift. And it is for you, too.

Committing to yourself

Committing to yourself is a prerequisite for alonement. If getting to know yourself doesn't hold much value for you, then time alone is wasted time. Yet, I suspect you *do* want to get to know yourself a little better. Maybe you're at a time in your life where you feel some part of you has been neglected and you're not quite sure how it happened. Perhaps you live an extremely sociable life, yet you feel that, curiously, it isn't quite *enough* – something, somewhat imperceptibly, is missing.

Initially, my journey of self-commitment was prompted by the biggest cliché imaginable: a break-up. I'd moved out of my best friend's flat into my own place, living alone for the first time in my life. Shortly afterwards, my relationship with my boyfriend – who had all but moved in – ended, at a time when the majority of my friends were in serious relationships. Two of my childhood best friends moved in with their respective boyfriends and then, within the same month, got engaged. My brother – who had previously guarded his love life like a government secret – met his Serious Girlfriend. I couldn't relate when my friends gushed about having 'someone to come home to', and I was a fifth wheel at family dinners. Oh, and a year later, when I thought I'd finally got a handle on all this extra time alone, there was a worldwide pandemic to throw into the mix.

In this strange, reconfigured world, I was literally more 'alone' than ever before. Nothing, and I mean nothing, tops off eight days of quarantine like a Zoom quiz where you're the only team of one, with sixteen different households of couples or flatmates staring back at you. Being alone is all fun and games until you attempt to answer the 'Sport' category All By Yourself (if the answer wasn't David Beckham, I was quite literally clueless). Before you present me with the world's tiniest violin, let me stop you there. Through being more physically isolated than ever, I was forced to confront my fear of being alone; and to commit, more meaningfully than ever, to myself.

Before I go into all that, I want to call time on the notion that break-ups are the *only* reason for committing to yourself. OK, sure – break-ups *can* be a ripe time for self-discovery (see *The Holiday*, *Eat Pray Love*, *Legally Blonde* and/or read up on Miley Cyrus's relationship history for further evidence). There's a certain logic to this; losing a partner can feel like losing a limb, and drastic action (i.e. self-discovery) can seem necessary to fill that void. Psychologists have identified the profound 'reduced self-concept clarity' that can come with a relationship breakdown. 'Not only may couples come to complete each others' sentences, they may actually come to complete each others' selves,' observes psychologist Erica B. Slotter.*

But here's a radical thought: how about treating self-commitment as more than just a fallback option? What if you don't need a messy heartbreak in order to 'find yourself'? What if committing to yourself could be a *thing*, regardless of whether or not you are in a couple? Emma Watson was right on the money with her 'self-partnered' status back in November 2019, prompting ridicule, masturbation jokes and, latterly, thought-provoking conversations about what it might mean to partner yourself. As she clarified, being self-partnered has nothing to do with your official romantic status. 'For me it's much more about your relationship with yourself and the feeling that you're not somehow deficient, in some way, because you aren't with someone,' she told *E! News* in December 2019.†

---

* Erica B. Slotter et al., 'Who Am I Without You? The Influence of Romantic Breakup on the Self-Concept', *Personality and Social Psychology Bulletin* (2009). https://journals.sagepub.com/doi/10.1177/0146167209352250

† Cydney Contreras, 'Emma Watson Is "So Happy" People Feel Empowered by her "Self-Partnered" Label'. *E! News* 10 December 2019. https://www.eonline.com/uk/news/1101124/emma-watson-is-so-happy-people-feel-empowered-by-her-self-partnered-label

Yet you're still left with the question of: *when?* When do you consciously make the decision to commit to yourself if there's no clear trigger? Curiously, we live in a society preoccupied with celebrating weddings and childbirth, but there are few rituals centred around celebrating our lifelong commitment to ourselves. It's perhaps this value system that has inspired some to turn marital commitment on its head; and marry themselves. This symbolic (i.e. not legally binding) ritual is known as sologamy. Sophie Tanner, author of *Reader, I Married Me!*, took the plunge in 2015 after – you guessed it – a messy break-up. She says: 'I woke up one morning and my sense of self had come back. I had this realisation that I really liked myself, my job, and my life in Brighton. I had this sense of security where I don't need anyone but myself to be responsible for my own happiness.'

While self-marriage is certainly not for everyone, the message of radical self-love is an inspiring one. Tanner, who has continued to date other people since tying the knot with herself five years ago, says: 'I wanted to commit to a sense of happiness in myself. In western society we don't have any personal development rituals to mark that.' Stories like Tanner's are served up on the news cycle every few years, and quite quickly become the stuff of mockery. Tanner herself says she was trolled online after photos of her special day hit the headlines. It's not hard to see why people take issue with the idea of sologamy; some might question the need to apply the convention of marriage – historically conducted for economic and religious purposes – around a relationship with oneself. Others might think it excessive or narcissistic to have a huge ceremony *just* for oneself. Usually these ceremonies involve some cost, and spending this money might not seem affordable (or relatable) as a single person. Some might just deem it bonkers.

Yet, putting all that aside, the process remains an intriguing one – because when else do we openly affirm our relationship with ourselves? In *Sex and the City*, Carrie Bradshaw, tired of perpetually celebrating other people's life choices at wedding and baby showers, jokingly announces that she is marrying herself. She leaves her friend a voicemail: 'It's Carrie Bradshaw. I wanted to let you know that I'm getting married. To myself. I'm registered at Manolo Blahnik.' And, although she does this in the name of funding her designer shoe habit (what else?), Carrie justifies her decision, saying: 'If I don't ever get married or have a baby? . . . Think about it: If you are single, after graduation, there isn't one occasion where people celebrate you . . . I am talking about the single gal. Hallmark doesn't make a "Congratulations you didn't marry the wrong guy" card.'*

In the absence of meaningful ways to mark self-commitment, it's very, very easy for it to slide down your list of priorities. More urgent, it seems, are your grandma's

---

* Season 6, episode 9, *Sex and the City*, 'A Woman's Right to Shoes', created by Darren Starr, written by Jenny Bicks, produced by HBO.

weekly phone calls to ask whether you've 'found a boyfriend yet' or, if you do have a partner, the question of 'where things are going', and it's tempting to file away the task of committing to yourself for a later date. And yet – even in the absence of social cues – it's important to remember that you are a priority. You don't need to marry yourself. You don't even have to be going steady. But I have, instead, a modest proposal for you: factor quality time alone into your daily life. Whether that's sitting down for a cup of tea without your phone or going for a walk, these actions demonstrate a continued commitment to yourself.

You could be at a perfectly stable point in your life, or in what feels like a crisis. You could be single, or perfectly happy in your relationship. You could be living on a farm in rural Iceland, or in a house-share in Manchester. There doesn't need to be a dramatic moment in your life that makes you acknowledge your aloneness, simply because you have *always* been alone; and, while you may not have recognised them, your needs, your curiosity, your deeper purpose, have always been there, waiting quietly in the wings. You are used to committing time and energy to those people you consider valuable, so make yourself one of them. Once you value your connection to yourself, you commit, first and foremost, to the notion that you are important.

First stop: Alonement

True commitment, as any long-term couple will know, is demonstrated by what you do in the day to day, not in grand gestures or big ceremonies. All that is really necessary in order to commit to yourself is to commit to spend time alone and to learn to do it well. I'm biased, of course, but I think buying this book is a good first step.

Of course, it's being alone *well* – that's the crux of it, not simply being alone. Through actively and mindfully learning to value spending time alone, you begin a process of investing in *you*: your self-growth, your self-care, your inner world. You normalise it for other people, who both respect your need for alone time and begin to think more consciously about their own (because alonement is contagious in the best possible way). You're devoting time and energy to the person you'll spend the rest of your life with. And you know what? That's someone worth getting to know.

2

GETTING TO KNOW *YOU*

In 2015, a tweet from Jason Gay (@JasonGay), a sports columnist at *The Wall Street Journal*, went viral: 'There's a guy in this coffee shop sitting at the table, not on his phone, not on a laptop. Just drinking coffee, like a psychopath.'

The tweet, which sparked a whole host of internet memes, may have been tongue-in-cheek, but it proved a sad indictment of our times. It's become more 'normal' than not to be plugged into a digital world rather than mindfully enjoying the here and now. For me, it's less relevant that the so-called Coffee Shop Psychopath was alone in a public space (Chapter 6 is devoted to the value of feeling you deserve to occupy so-called public spaces alone). I reckon the Coffee Shop Psychopath tweet is more of an ironic reflection on The Way We Live Now, where it's more relatable to joke that someone's a 'psychopath' for sitting alone with their thoughts rather than questioning the psychological shortcomings of not being able to. I know, I know, internet memes become so much funnier when you butcher them through analysis.

The ability to be content in one's own mind – even just for a short while – is a key part of learning to spend time alone. Yet it's gained a sort of oddball (or superpower, depending on how you see it) status in modern-day western society, which offers a whole host of other alternatives. When you think about it, it shouldn't be such an anomaly to see someone sipping coffee alone and undistracted, but it clearly unsettles us to see someone content in their own company. Maybe that's because it reminds us, somewhat inconveniently, of what we're just not very good at.

The fear of one's own thoughts isn't an exclusively 21st-century phenomenon. French writer Sidonie-Gabrielle Colette, who published under the pseudonym Colette, wrote in 1908: 'There are days when solitude is a heady wine that intoxicates you with freedom, others when it is a bitter tonic, and still others when it is a poison that makes you beat your head against the wall.' The electric shock study I mentioned in the Introduction – where a majority of study participants chose to give themselves electric shocks rather than sit calmly in silence for 15 minutes – sort of drives home the point. 'Discomfort' is a word that comes up time and time again when people talk about being alone with their own thoughts. While the amount of discomfort varies, it's safe to assume it outweighs, for many of us, the sensation of a small electric shock.

As I write this, I'm reminded of a brilliant scene in *Peep Show* where Mark, played by David Mitchell, teaches his flatmate Jez, played by Robert Webb, how to concentrate on reading *Wuthering Heights*. Jez, who's only ever read *Mr Nice*, has committed to the cause in order to impress a woman he fancies.

Jez: I look at it, I read the words or think I do, but then I get distracted, and I don't quite take it in, and I have to go back. I've been on the same four pages for three hours. Mark, how do you read? Can you teach me how to read? How do you concentrate? Please tell me.

Mark: Well turn the telly off for a start. Start reading that long paragraph there. You probably feel like looking away from the page now, don't you?

Jez: *[Shaking]* Yes, yes, I do.

Mark: Don't look away. Stay with it.

Jez: *[Still trembling]* Oh, it's too difficult! *[Slams down the book]**

Technology gives us an easy way out of this struggle. Even

---

* Season 7, episode 3, *Peep Show*, 'A Beautiful Mind', written by Simon Black-well, produced by Objective Media Group.

in the absence of other people, we're increasingly able to escape ourselves digitally – and perhaps this has never been quite so prevalent as it became during lockdown. As much as digital connectivity was and is a lifeline (living alone, it was my entire social life for a couple of months), it can also be a leash. Many of us found ourselves 'doomscrolling' – a term that describes purposefully seeking out bleak, depressing news – while others found themselves obsessively checking Twitter or swiping on dating apps (on 29 March 2020, when most of the world was in lockdown, Tinder recorded three billion swipes worldwide – an all-time record).* More than once, during the first days of lockdown, my iPhone screen time total was more than a contracted 9–5 working day.

Pandemic or not, the temptation to escape uncomfortable thoughts is rife. I don't just mean diagnosed phobias or trauma – it can be as simple as a minor inconvenience. Often, if I encounter a work-related issue or know I have to have an awkward conversation with someone, I'll find myself scrolling Instagram. I'm not entirely sure why my brain makes this connection (you'd have to ask Mark Zuckerberg), but it certainly doesn't solve any of my problems. These emotional crutches distract us from the need to take action in our lives – and they aren't the only culprits.

---

* Dougal Shaw, 'Coronavirus: Tinder boss says "dramatic" changes to dating'. *BBC News*, 21 May 2020. https://www.bbc.co.uk/news/business-52743454

A golden age of distraction

Not a fan of the whole introspection thing? Don't worry; you don't have to be. Here's the à la carte menu of distractions:

Entrées

- Listening to music
- Running
- Gaming
- Reading
- Going to the gym
- Watching TV
- Shopping
- Obsessing over romantic interest(s)
- Checking Twitter
- Doomscrolling
- Checking your email

Main course

Comfort eating £0.89
   A pack of digestives with a coulis of self-loathing

Alcohol. £7.99
   A cocktail of vodka, tonic and ill-advised behaviour

Scrolling Instagram .... Free
*Flank steak of fitness model, accompanied by a side
of poached ego*

WhatsApp .... £220 pp
A stew of hen party politics, served piping hot

Dessert

- Drugs
- Gambling
- Sex
- Smoking

Choose your poison.

The beauty of living in the 21st century is that you can quite conveniently opt out of feeling your feelings, and there are a number of socially acceptable ways to do it. Most of us rarely go anywhere without our phone. People overlap relationships so they're never single, or spend every moment with their housemates, or commit almost every waking hour of the day to being 'at work' (either physically or virtually, via Gmail and Slack). Ever heard of eating your feelings? We can eat, smoke or drink our way through every challenging emotion.

We find creative and, in many cases, perfectly inoffensive, ways to escape our thoughts. You would never think of someone as insane for checking their phone every two minutes, or working past midnight, or arranging Hinge dates every free weeknight. Socially, we look down on drug addicts or alcoholics, all the while pretending we're not battling an addiction in a comparable (albeit more socially acceptable) way. We curse our butterfly-brains and our TikTok addiction but continue to ignore what we actually need to address. Such is the nature of modern-day life that we're unlikely to spend much time *really* alone unless we actively seek it out: going for a solitary swim, staring at a wall, meditating, journalling. Or, you know, sitting in a café just drinking coffee. Like a psychopath.

The entrance fee to alonement

We've got to a place where so many of us are not on speaking terms with our innermost thoughts, and that's a problem – not least because sitting with your own thoughts is a basic requirement for alonement. I don't mean hour upon hour of rumination. No one's telling you to go and sit alone on a rock in the middle of the Brecon Beacons. Hell, even I don't want to go and sit alone on a rock in the middle of the Brecon Beacons. So here are some more achievable, everyday alternatives:

- Walk the 20 minutes to your nearest train station without headphones on.

- Spend the first hour of your day without looking at your phone.
- Ban yourself from snacking for a day.
- Disable WhatsApp during working hours.
- Go for a night out without drinking.

Baby steps, maybe, but you may well be surprised by how uncomfortable you find following these not-so-radical suggestions, as you begin to feel your feelings instead of drowning them. Interestingly, this is something so many of us were forced to do in the depths of lockdown. With so many of our typical offline distractions, from shopping in person to socialising, holidays and clubbing, off the cards for a while, it seems that tech (after a few ill-advised eight-hour stints) did not ultimately suffice as a distraction, and we were forced to introspect – for better or for worse.

The good news is that, once you start practising tuning in to your own thoughts, you open yourself up to a whole lot of fringe benefits. To take a handful, you'll start to:

- Think consciously and positively about what you want to do with your alone time
- Maintain a sense of self outside of your relationships
- Reveal the creative potential of being in your own mind
- Experience 'flow' in activities you love

- Enjoy situations that will inevitably entail *some substantial* time in your own head, like going to a restaurant alone or solo travel
- Retreat – peacefully and comfortably – into the sanctuary of your own mind, even in busy scenarios. (On my Alonement podcast, former *Blue Peter* presenter and children's author Konnie Huq said she's able to 'be alone' in her own mind. If that isn't a superpower, I don't know what is.)

Sounds compelling, doesn't it? Now for the bad news. Sadly, the process often isn't as clear-cut as simply being alone with your own thoughts and realising, 'Hey, this isn't so bad!' Like cold-water swimming, sitting with your own thoughts often involves not just jumping in, but also thrashing around for a bit until you warm up. Psychologist Shahroo Izadi agrees with me. She describes sitting with your own thoughts as 'the first step in reframing being alone'. Yet she acknowledges that, once you opt for the 'own thoughts' tasting menu rather than the à la carte of distractions, things can get tricky. That's because actively embracing discomfort can 'turn up the volume' on what you were scared of addressing in the first place: your anxieties or doubts.

Someone I found hugely inspiring on this subject was public-school-girl-turned-explosive-ordnance-disposal-expert-turned-*Love Island*-contestant Camilla Thurlow, whom I interviewed for the podcast. As you might guess from

Camilla's somewhat eclectic CV, she has actively sought out uncomfortable situations throughout her life – even if that has meant some serious soul-searching. During work assignments in Afghanistan and Zimbabwe, she was frequently the only woman and could only communicate through a translator. 'When there was friction or difficulty or discomfort, it made me feel closer to myself. It gave me a situation where I had to learn more about who I was and what I could do,' she said. What amazed me about Camilla was not only how she consciously sought out situations that challenged her – but also how she embraced the self-inter-rogation that came with it, along with the fear and doubt of making a change in her life. 'I think it's important that we try and separate that fear of wrong decision-making from just having the option to learn a bit more about yourself and change direction,' she said. 'Surely we should be far more afraid of sticking with a decision that's wrong and just blindly following it through.' And that's just it; because always running away from this introspection means, inev-itably, limiting what you get out of life.

So, even if you see absolutely no value in alonement – say you've accidentally picked up your flatmate's copy of this book and have zero intention of following through with any of my other advice – I urge you to at least tackle the business of sitting with your own thoughts. There's no easy escape from tough emotions. There simply isn't. So many of us make the perfectly understandable decision not to hear them. Not today. Not this week. Possibly not *ever*. We feel the dull ache of inadequacy for years rather than confront the fact that we're jealous of a sibling or a best friend. We suffer sexual problems throughout every relationship rather than acknowledge what happened in our past. I could go on forever, but you get my gist. There's a long list of casualties. We compromise our whole lives because we just can't bear to hear ourselves, simply because it feels *so* uncomfortable, with all the little voices in your head out to get you. And, long term, the consequences can be so much worse than just discomfort. Running away from your thoughts is *ruinous*, even if no one else ever tells you that. In the words of Noel Gallagher, it's time to slip inside the eye of your mind.

Meet your inner critic

The first stop in our journey of self-exploration can often be a pretty unsavoury one, and that's because we come head-to-head with our so-called 'inner critic'. The inner critic, or critical inner voice, is a term used in popular psychology. It has its roots in psychoanalytic concepts such as the superego resistance (Freud) and the negative anima/animus (Jung). I guess 'inner critic' was catchier.

Anyway, the inner critic is a voice inside your head telling you negative or unhelpful things. These tend to have certain themes depending on the individual. Mine, for instance, likes to serenade me with less-than-inspiring comments such as: *You're not a good writer. You aren't able to finish this BODYCOMBAT class. You have no coordination. You're not artistic.* At worst: *You're an idiot. You're too much. Your Bolognese recipe isn't as good as you think it is.*

I talked to my friends about this, who admitted their inner critics said things like: *You're disorganised, you're a mess, you're fat, you're skinny, you're not creative, you're socially awkward, you're not funny, you have short legs, you're unpopular, you make no sense, your English isn't good enough, you're not good enough, everyone else is better than you, you're boring.*

Who's responsible for saying these horrible things? Really – everybody and nobody. That is to say, our inner critic tends to be a multi-faced mash-up of different people we've met during our lives, particularly our formative years. Izadi says, 'I've had people say it's from a series of sources, including parents, teachers and peers in formative years, magazines, films, ex-partners . . .' Add to the mix: childhood bullies, siblings, toxic friends, that Zara sales assistant who once gave you a funny look, the guy you met at Be At One that night, the girl from your university halls. It's a strange quirk of our brains that we will internalise negative comments made by these people and filter out all the good.

Personally, I used to struggle to acknowledge that I had an inner critic – even after I started to spend more time alone and began tuning in to the occasional unhelpful thoughts floating around in my head. I rationalised that I had a loving family, close friends and a good education, so who was I, with all those privileges, to have a negative inner voice? I was just like most people, it turns out. *Having* an inner critic isn't a failure – not by you or whoever raised you. In fact, it's more common than not to have one, according to therapist Sally Baker. 'It's believed some people have an inner cheerleader, instead – but I never meet those people,' says Baker. 'I've had clients who run national banks, or look like a million dollars, and are still dominated by their inner critics.' (Incidentally, if you are one of these mythical inner cheerleader people, I hereby award you a fast-track pass through this chapter.)

As Baker suggests, our actions are influenced profoundly by this inner critic, which acts 'like a drip, drop of toxic rain' and usually below our conscious awareness. It's the voice that will make you slip up in job interviews, even when you're more than qualified for the role and have spent a whole week preparing. It's the voice that makes you sabotage your relationship by 'testing' your partner. It's the voice your boot camp fitness class instructor will tell you to ignore on the third round of burpees – but you still cave into it.

Often, our inner critical voice is a self-fulfilling prophecy. I challenge anyone, for instance, to be funny if their inner critic is telling them they're not funny, or to dance well if their inner critic is telling them they can't dance. We tell ourselves we can't, so we don't, and so reinforce our doubtful and negative self-perception. If you're constantly distracted (see above for menu of available options), then you're much less likely to consciously 'hear' this inner critic. But this doesn't mean it's not influencing you. 'In a sense, you're making the inner critic's job remarkably easy, because it gets "free rein" over your mind,' Baker explains. In other words, if we don't go through the formality of meeting our inner critic, we remain controlled by them.

Time alone is a surefire way of turning the volume up on this inner critic. When we're alone, those niggling negative statements get louder. Inside your mind lies a deep, dark well of pain – and, on some level, we all know this. So, reasonably, we avoid time alone, because – let's face it – that inner critic doesn't sound like someone you want to spend time with.

Hold up. Isn't this a book that advocates spending *more* time alone? Yes. About that. Spending time alone will, for many of us, come with an unwelcome side serving of discomfort, particularly if we're not used to it. Unsurprisingly, the harsher your inner critic, the more you'll try to escape from it. But you know what? You should confront it anyway. I'm aware that what I'm suggesting here is a particularly hard sell. But it is, I believe, a worthy one – for two reasons. Firstly, because standing up to your inner critic is pretty tantamount to living yo' best life. Secondly, because – a subject close to my heart – it's only through learning to hear and stand up to your inner critic that you can comfortably spend time by yourself. It may seem like a steep entrance fee, but I promise it's worth it.

Becoming a friend to yourself

Still reading? Good.

Thankfully, the inner critic isn't the only voice available in our heads. We're also able to foster another voice: that of an inner friend. *Not*, I want to stress, the friend who sends you pass-agg WhatsApps late at night, nor the one who gets *so* drunk every single night out that you spend the whole night looking after them, every bloody time. It's the friend who sends you a little card in the post when you get promoted at work, or randomly tells you how glowing your skin is looking. *Your inner cheerleader.*

Some people talk about this as 'self-compassion'. In her book *Self Compassion*, Dr Kristin Neff explains the importance of showing kindness and sympathy to oneself as you might another person. She writes: 'When we give ourselves compassion, the knot of negative self-judgement starts to dissolve, replaced by a feeling of peaceful, connected acceptance.' Then there's the ubiquitous 'self-love', which, of course, is honed almost exclusively through practising daily yoga, attending gong baths and posting about it on Instagram.

Personally, when I think about befriending myself, I prefer to start with the gentler and somewhat less intimidating goal of, simply, liking myself. It's less about writing sonnets to your stretch marks or saying affirmations in the mirror (as much as both these things can be good), and more about showing myself curiosity, understanding and kindness – the qualities I would want to extend to a friend. You might not be ready for a radical and visible act of self-love, but can you *like* yourself a little more today?

This friendly voice in your head might say things like: *That's an interesting thought. You worked really hard at the gym today. You've got a headache, you should probably drink some water. You deserve a nap.* It also allows you to be curious about yourself and to give weight to the things you care about: *Hey, you should Shazam that song. What was that book you wanted to read? It's been a while since you practised your Italian – maybe you should download Duolingo.* Once we hone this inner friend, we're capable of listening to this vastly more encouraging voice instead. We speak back to our negative, intrusive thoughts, diminishing their power. *You didn't mess up during that meeting; didn't you notice the client was really engaged and asked lots of questions? Your boyfriend isn't losing interest in you, he's probably just stressed with work this week. You aren't fat, you're a perfectly healthy weight.*

As Daisy Buchanan said on the podcast: 'I realised that my brain doesn't have to talk to me the way it wants to. I can choose how I think, I can give myself really good advice. I don't have to come to everything with a terrible mental soundtrack.'

As you nurture your inner friend and learn to like yourself, you become more and more adept at moving outside of the boundaries imposed by your self-doubt. You will learn not to simply absorb what your inner critic is saying, but to answer back, and contradict, instead. You'll begin to talk to yourself, rather than listen to yourself. And you know what? It's empowering as hell. Try it before your next fitness class or before a difficult presentation and see what a difference it makes.

'But my friends know me better than I know myself'

At this point, you might want to butt in and say: isn't it enough to have, er, real-life friends to speak to when I'm feeling insecure or demoralised? Sadly, no. Not even if you have the *best friends ever.* No offence to them.

Sometimes, we'll say of our friends, partners or family members that they know us better than we know ourselves, but this is actually problematic. Don't get me wrong; it's a joy and a privilege to know someone else so intimately that you can sometimes read their thoughts. My best friends and I (and yes, they are *the best friends ever*) sometimes joke that we can 'have a poke around' in one another's brains, because we've become so good at deciphering one another's thoughts after well over a decade of friendship. One of them breathes ever so slightly faster when she's bored, whereas another one does a tell-tale head tilt when she's trying to schmooze people (it's actually adorable). Yet, inevitably, the person you have the greatest potential insight into, and control over, will always be yourself – living, as you do, in your own head. I say *potential* insight, because it's often not a given that we *do* know ourselves better than our friends. As we know, we live in an age of connectivity, where we can outsource our emotional processing at the touch of a button.

A caveat: I'm so grateful to have close friends who will a) listen to my problems, and b) offer a different perspective, and I love being that person for them too. But, outside of an actual emergency (for instance, after a break-up that shatters every semblance of emotional resilience), I try to roll things around in my own head first and then speak to them about it, rather than dumping everything unedited on WhatsApp. These are some of the messages I've sent to friends in the past:

I'm so nervous about the job interview
I'm feeling insecure today
My boss literally hates me
OMG I've eaten SO much

It's fine to share, but I probably could have talked myself up internally, too – particularly when I wasn't exactly looking for practical external support. It's not that we shouldn't speak to our friends about our problems; it's just that if we immediately outsource every tough emotion that ever crosses our mind, any capacity for emotional regulation goes straight out the window. We become entirely dependent on others to silence our inner critic. Time alone becomes ever more unappealing, because we don't actually have the internal resources to *cope* alone.

We have gotten out of the habit of digesting our emotions and summoning our inner friend, because another, inevitably less informed, source is, quite literally, at our fingertips. We'll let our friends swipe through our Tinder apps and consult on our break-ups and console us about the latest work drama, all the while refusing to acknowledge that we have the autonomy to change and influence our own lives. We are in the driver's seat, but we prefer to defer to the person in the back because we're not used to exercising self-control. And this should never be the norm. Daisy made an important point about this self-reliance in the podcast: 'No one ever is going to give me the advice or feedback or praise or love that I crave, I've got to give that to myself.'

Like many people, communicating with friends and family during lockdown made me even more aware of the impact that emotional dumping can have on others. Everyone around me was going through something – job losses, furlough, relationship issues, loneliness, general anxiety and even bereavement in some tragic circumstances. Knowing how much everyone was navigating at once meant that my capacity for emotional self-soothing increased – and I learnt to be a trusted friend to myself.

Becoming a friend to yourself doesn't mean never turning to your other friends. Sometimes, they will have experience beyond yours that might help to inform your decisions; for instance, a close friend recently entered the world of online dating, and a few weeks in, she turned to me – a veteran – to ask my opinion on her approach (as it happens, I think this is one of those areas where you don't really benefit all that much from 'experience' – better to go in fresh, excited and authentically yourself, rather than jaded by a few years of swiping). The thing is, you can't really absorb advice without knowing your own mind first, which means rolling things around in your head a little and hearing your own feelings first. I know it's hard. But I promise you, you're stronger and more capable than you think.

Journalling: Meeting yourself on paper

Struggling to make sense of your thoughts? Try journaling. I could write a whole book on the power of this practice. Hell, in writing my diary over the years I practically have (although God knows no one would publish it).

Let's get one thing straight. In my opinion, there are no rules. You can write in your journal once a week, or every day at 9.03pm. You can use a battered old notebook, or a specialised journal formatted with different sections for your to do list, your daily affirmation and the three things you're grateful for. You can write in rhyming couplets or do away with punctuation altogether. Honestly, whatever works. You do *you*.

This is what my diary-writing process looks like. I have three notebooks: a 'morning' notebook from Papier, a marbled gratitude journal, and a yellow Moleskine that lives on my bedside table. The morning notebook is for taking stock before a tough day of work and identifying my aims and struggles. I'm freelance these days, so it's a bit like having a morning meeting with myself, without the need for Zoom or small talk. But it's the Moleskine, for evening time, that tends to get the most love. After filling in my 'three things I'm grateful for' in the gratitude journal, I'll typically write a stream-of-consciousness about whatever's weighing on my mind in my yellow diary, before bed, about three or four times a week. Sometimes I'll neglect it for a couple of days if something intense is happening, and I'll feel it summoning me: *we need to talk.*

I've written a diary on and off my whole life, taking gaps of a few years which have often coincided with romantic relationships, but two years ago I made it a non-negotiable. Since then, journalling has been the most consistent ritual for my mental health (and there's a fair amount of research behind this, with one study* showing that simply putting a name to your feelings helps reduce the intensity of your emotional response, making you feel less sad or angry). Writing a journal is how I've really learnt to become a friend to myself. It is a fundamental part of my alonement, and I urge you to follow suit.

Writing a diary forces you to feel your feelings, and once they're out, you can deal with them. You take a step back and see your thoughts – including those that come from your inner critic – for what they really are. As you write your daily account you might think, *Am I really an inadequate piece of sh*t who will never amount to anything, or did I simply make a one-off mistake at work today because I was tired?* You become the sympathetic ear to yourself that you previously only extended to your loved ones. And as you habitually practise self-compassion on paper, it filters into the voice in your head, too. Your self-esteem blossoms, both by virtue of the kind things you've told yourself, and the fact that you have continuously committed to showing up for yourself. It keeps you accountable to the inner hopes and dreams that your inner critic regularly shouts down. Over time, it allows me to build a core of me-ness: a joined-up self, a narrative thread connecting my days and the personal development

---

* University of California Los Angeles, 'Putting Feelings Into Words Produces Therapeutic Effects In The Brain', *Science Daily*, 22 June 2007. https://www.sciencedaily.com/releases/2007/06/070622090727.htm

that runs alongside them. Writing my journal is when I feel most in tune with myself.

A lot of people swear by Julia Cameron's 'morning pages' approach to journalling, introduced in her bestselling book, *The Artist's Way: A Course in Discovering and Recovering Your Creative Self*. 'Morning pages' isn't just a catchy name; Cameron means it *very* literally. 'Put simply, the morning pages are three pages of longhand writing, strictly stream-of-consciousness.' They also have to be done first thing in the morning, and you're not allowed to 'skip or skimp' on them. Apart from these (rather strict!) ground rules, there is 'no wrong way to do morning pages', plus, crucially, you do not have to be a 'writer' to do them.

Technically, Cameron's method is for creative people to remove creative blocks: 'All that angry, whiny, petty stuff . . . worrying about the job, the laundry, the funny knock in the car, the weird look in your lover's eye', but, as many have discovered, it's a universally applicable model for journalling in general – whether or not you think you have a 'novel in you'. Morning pages can prove useful in navigating your relationships; parenting; work; any kind of self-development. Cameron even taps into the idea of the inner friend versus inner critic; she calls her handy inner friend 'Little Julie' (cute!) while she refers to her inner critic by the less adorable title of 'the Censor'. Her advice for overcoming your inner critic: 'Make this a rule: always remember that your Censor's negative opinions are not the truth. This takes practice. By spilling out of bed and straight onto the page every morning, you learn to evade the Censor.'

I don't do morning pages – not in *The Artist's Way* sense, anyway. (Don't tell Julia Cameron.) But given that the likes of Elizabeth Gilbert, Russell Brand and Kerry Washington (how's *that* for a fantasy dinner party line-up?) are all fans of Cameron's, it's definitely worth a try – particularly if you don't consider yourself particularly creative. Plus, hers is a useful argument about how designating alonement time can help you overcome those pesky negative thoughts.

I want to suggest, albeit reluctantly, that journalling may not be for everyone. Although anecdotally it seems like a pretty failsafe methodology, some simply don't feel the need for it; a close friend of mine says she finds it easier to reflect inside her own head. Others may find it actively unhelpful: there was a study in 2012 that found those using journalling as a tool after a divorce found it increased negative rumination;* although bizarrely, another study five years later seemed to directly contradict those results.† In any case, if you do find journalling unhelpful, here are some alternatives.

---

* Association for Psychological Science, 'Post-divorce journalling may hinder healing for some', *Science Daily*, 29 November 2012. https://www.sciencedaily.com/releases/2012/11/121129143500.htm

† Wolters Kluwer Health, '"Narrative expressive writing" might protect against harmful health effects of divorce-related stress', *Science Daily*, 8 May 2017. https://www.sciencedaily.com/releases/2017/05/170508162304.htm

Mindfulness and meditation

Mindfulness is about bringing conscious awareness to the present moment, or, in blunter terms, simply focusing on doing one thing at a time, while meditation is any activity you do mindfully (so, not just sitting closed-eyed in a lotus position, but we'll get to that). Although journalling overlaps with meditation in some ways – for instance, it requires you to focus on one activity and sit with your thoughts – it doesn't quite work as a substitute. That's because, when you're journalling, you're not clearing your mind or being still – there's a sense of working through something, beavering through your problems with an air of emotional admin.

We are meditating when we practise mindfulness during small, everyday tasks. Take potato peeling, a two-handed, immersive, and – yes – meditative task. It's not about analysing the potato, or empathising with the potato, or even being at one with the potato. It's about being comfortable enough to reside in your mind as you focus on the task in front of you – and not to run away from that, or any feelings that might come with it.

I didn't realise this when I first came across mindfulness, while I was working at a popular health and fitness magazine as a full-time guinea pig and occasional writer. I initially went down the route of many others, struggling to commit to the basic ten minutes of one-on-one time listening to Andy Puddicombe on Headspace, and eventually I put mindfulness in the category of chia seeds, coconut water and reformer Pilates. Zeitgeist-y, but not for me. A few months ago, as I stood outside Chalk Farm tube station, red-faced and melting after a BODYCOMBAT class, I bumped into an old friend, who appeared to be floating down the road towards me with an aura of calm so intense that it practically enveloped me as I stopped him to say hello. It turns out he was doing walking meditation, and our conversation reminded me that mindfulness can be applied to almost everything – be it peeling potatoes, walking to the train station or applying your make-up.

It took me a while to understand how mindfulness related to alonement. Sure, it's something you do when you're physically alone, but I reasoned that 'emptying the mind' took you away from your own thoughts rather than connecting you to them. How did that compare to my beloved journalling practice, where I proactively confronted everything in my head with the air of a boxer entering a ring?

Journalling is great, but it turns out there's also inherent value in learning to sit with emotions and not do anything about them. You can't spend every moment carefully untangling your mind – you have to allow for its tangledness and co-exist with it. These feelings often accompany the things we challenge ourselves to do. Let's say you decide to go for sushi by yourself – as I will challenge all of you to do in Chapter 6 – and you feel uneasy without a friend to choose a table with. Learning to sit with that feeling of unease (rather than responding to it by leaving the café or looking at your phone) is key to moving you forward and turning that solo experience into alonement. What's more – mindfulness allows you to feel the positive feelings, too. When you're alone, your experience isn't filtered through the perspective of the person you're with; it's all on you, pal. This is why being mindfully in the moment is pretty damn essential for alonement.

Therapy and coaching

Everyone is different, and it could be that certain negative thought patterns are so ingrained that it requires another person to help you reprogramme the way your mind works. Yes, ultimately alonement is about learning to spend time alone and to do it well, but that doesn't mean you have to go through that journey exclusively by yourself. Mental health campaigner and author Jonny Benjamin spoke on my Alonement podcast about how talking therapy had helped him overcome the 'negative catastrophising thoughts' that accompanied his alone time. While once this time had descended into 'guilt, escapism, drinking by myself', it is now something Jonny is able to actively seek out for positive reasons.

Other psychological interventions for recurring negative thought processes include cognitive behavioural therapy (CBT), which helps people to recognise their negative thought patterns and stop giving power to them. This is often done through learning to separate themselves from their emotions – *I am experiencing fear right now* – or a compassion-based approach: *what would I say if I were talking to a friend?* Typically, CBT comes in the form of professional help, which takes place over between 12 and 20 one-hour sessions and can be prescribed privately or by the NHS. There's also neuro-linguistic programming (NLP), a newer technique aimed at tackling specific psychological traumas and diminishing the power those memories have over us – which might prove useful for those facing specific abandonment issues associated with being alone. NLP is currently only available privately, costing between £60 and £100 a session.*

Reaping rewards

Often, we think of being alone as a physical state, but, when it comes to alonement, the ability to be comfortable in your own mind is just as fundamental. As I mentioned at the beginning of this chapter, it's normal to escape your 'aloneness' even when you're without company – but that doesn't mean it's right. Alonement can be a restorative, reflective time where you hear all the good stuff in your mind – your

---

* 'NLP Practitioner', *Reed.co.uk*. https://www.reed.co.uk/courses/nlp-practitioner/ 22964

imagination, your curiosity, your gratitude, your sensory experience of the world – but only if you actively guide yourself to make this happen.

However you choose to do it, I hope you agree that the challenge of being comfortable in your own mind is a worthy one. Making that head of yours a safe space won't always be easy, and I'll admit that it takes regular effort (the idea that you simply reach a fixed state of 'finding enlightenment' is a total myth). But no matter how hard it is, you'll reap life-changing rewards. So shove two fingers up at your inner critic, fight your demons and lean in to all the good stuff that comes from some time with me, myself and I.

3

DOING TIME (ALONE)

'You need to work on your solitude skills,' said no one, ever. We hear a lot about social skills, however: the tools we need to interact harmoniously with other people. Social skills involve communicating effectively with others, working well together, actively listening. Developing these skills is a key focus in so many areas of life, from early-years education to workplace bonding.

Social skills are shoved down our throats, whether or not we're particularly sociable people. The square peg, round hole metaphor certainly holds true here. Think of that episode of *Gilmore Girls*, where Rory Gilmore – perhaps one of television's finest depictions of an introvert – is told by her headteacher that she has to stop reading books at lunchtime and instead socialise with her classmates, in order to get a better recommendation letter for college. Yet as any fan of the show will know, Rory's capacity to retreat into a world of books – a typically 'introvert' characteristic – is simply fundamental to her personality, not to mention an improving academic habit that eventually leads her to be class valedictorian.

In the same way that social skills can be a struggle, a great number of us lack the ability to spend time alone in a meaningful, productive or enjoyable way. That's where solitude skills come in. Solitude skills – so termed by Dr Virginia Thomas, author of the paper 'How to be alone: An investigation of solitude skills'* – are the equivalent of social skills, but for time alone. They are what's needed to 'transform alone time into a positive solitude experience rather than an isolating, terrifying one'. A cause close to my heart.

Dr Thomas's work chimes with me because solitude skills are essentially your alonement toolkit. The ability to relish your alone time brings meaning and value to your life – and that's something that's rarely emphasised as a personal strength, in the same way that having great social skills is. Alexandra Shulman, former editor of British *Vogue*, values this lesser-celebrated skillset really highly. On my Alonement podcast, she said: 'I think one of the great talents in life is to be happy on your own. People who are content on their own,

---

* Virginia D. Thomas, 'How To Be Alone: An Investigation of Solitude Skills', June 2017. https://escholarship.org/uc/item/4gm0c2vq

who can also relate to other people, that is a great talent – because, at the end of the day, we are on our own really and it's important to be able to be on our own. I think it's also something that we don't value enough. It's a skill that's worth trying to perfect.'

Alone time, at its best, should be a self-actualising experience. It's a chance to do the activities you love, like exercise or pursuing a creative hobby. It's to get to know yourself, to recognise your ambitions and to look after yourself. In theory, great. The trouble is, if we lack 'solitude skills', often solo time can descend into the opposite.

Expectation: a bubble bath, a chilled glass of Sauvignon Blanc, a copy of *Middlemarch* and Radio 4 playing in the background, before changing into silk pyjamas and dancing around to 'Superfreak' like Cameron Diaz at the start of *Charlie's Angels.*

Reality: Falling down an Instagram rabbit hole, bingeing on Ben & Jerry's (plus whatever chocolate you find in the back of the cupboard) and texting your ex.

If your time spent alone looks more like the latter, then you will start to associate solitude with negative behaviour patterns that leave you feeling absolutely lousy. And I don't blame you; as you've probably already discovered, carving time out to be by yourself doesn't mean that – instantaneously, just like that – you're going to make the best of it. As Alain de Botton said on my podcast: 'It isn't enough to say you can know yourself from being alone, because there are ways of being alone that are actually not being with yourself.' While some people's preferred escapism is a ménage a trois with Ben & Jerry, Alain gave the example of someone obsessively scrolling through the news to avoid introspection. Whatever it is, we all have our unhealthy habits which can creep in while we're supposed to be having quality me-time. Maybe that's not surprising, given how many of us are so thoroughly unused to spending significant periods of time alone. What's more, we focus a lot, as we grow older, on learning how to develop 'social skills' for being in the company of others – but rarely take the same proactive, critical approach towards honing our ability to thrive when we're alone. So, is it any wonder that our 'solitude skills' are a little rusty?

Practising the art of being alone

In her research, Dr Thomas identifies eight solitude skills, which she divides into the categories of 'connection with self' and 'proactive'. Here are some of the 'solitude skills' we could all benefit from:

Connection with self	Proactive
Emotional regulation	Carving out time for solitude
Introspection	Negotiating with others for time in solitude
Noticing and heeding internal signals to enter solitude	Being mindful of how time in solitude was spent
Enjoyment of solitary activities	Balancing the needs for solitude and for sociability

Proactive skills largely focus around asserting your need for alone time in a sociable world: making time for yourself, negotiating this with others and making sure you don't end up as an insufferable hermit as a result. Depending on your life stage, proactive solitude can entail anything from taking yourself on a solo trip once a year to simply letting your friends know you're going off-grid for an afternoon to dig-ital-detox. Then, of course, there's parenthood. As Konnie Huq said on the podcast: 'Time to yourself changes as a mum. When you sit down with a cup of tea and they're just in the other room for two minutes, you learn to savour these precious moments.'

Thomas's 'connection with self' skills can require more soul-searching – particularly the emotional regulation and introspection aspects that we discussed in Chapter 2. Her 'proactive' solitude skills, listed in the table above, are about seizing the day – alone. Intriguingly, you could imagine a relationships counsellor applying similar principles when advising a struggling married couple. *Make time for each other. Think mindfully about the activities you're doing together. Balance quality time together with socialising.*

This approach makes sense. We make use of 'quality time' in order to get to know our loved ones better, so you shouldn't neglect quality time with yourself. In fact, I'd encourage you to apply the same principles you would when beginning a new relationship, or perhaps more accurately, reinvigorating an old one where the sex is non-existent and you've been sitting around on the sofa in your baked bean-stained pyjama bottoms a bit too much. If all this sounds like hard work, it should be. A good romantic relationship is worthy of making positive, proactive changes for: of 'injecting a bit of life' into. And so is your relationship with yourself.

To get you going, here are some of the 'solitude skills' I've developed myself.

Planning ahead – or not

Looking forward to things is one of the great joys in life. Doing this comes naturally to us when it concerns activities with other people; we'll say to someone we're dating, 'I can't wait to see you', or we'll while away time during a slow day at work Googling the online menu for the restaurant we're meeting friends at later on, or hotel reviews for our upcoming holiday. Anticipating a positive experience can boost your happiness long before the event has even taken place. A 2010 study* of Dutch adults unsurprisingly showed that those anticipating a holiday were, on average, much happier than those who didn't have one planned in the weeks or months ahead.

I'm with the Dutch social scientists on this one. As long as I can remember, I've always been an absolute sucker for having something to look forward to, and in the past I'd be very disappointed if these things didn't go to plan: if a boyfriend had to work late and cancelled our date night, for instance, or a hungover friend flaked on a brunch plan at the eleventh hour. It never occurred to me – back then – that I could do nice things, like going for a fancy meal or watching a film at the cinema, by myself.

My big epiphany about forward planning? 'Making plans' doesn't have to involve other people. Whether it's scheduling a night in for one or taking yourself to an exhibition that no one else wants to go to, you don't need another person in order to plan something to look forward to. You're allowed to diarise rewatching *When Harry Met Sally* while working on your crow pose in the same way

---

* Springer, 'Happiness is . . . looking forward to your vacation', *Science Daily*, 19 February 2010. https://www.sciencedaily.com/releases/2010/02/100218125204. htm

you do coffee with your friends. A plan with yourself is a valid plan.

Without applying this framework, periods of solitude can loom ahead as empty windows of time. This was a lesson I learnt while self-isolating alone during Covid-19, when I had no choice but to structure my life around activities I did with myself. I found it so much easier to leap out of bed if I'd downloaded a fun PopSugar dance video to give me a reason to wake up, while rebranding solo Friday nights in as 'movie nights' not only helped me ringfence my weekend, it also gave me a focus throughout the week exploring prospective film choices. Planning ahead reframes alone time as something joyful you'll look forward to. In her research project, Dr Thomas recommended her subjects take themselves out on 'solitude dates' planned up to three months in advance.

Planning ahead also means that you're likely to stick to whatever you've got planned for your solo time, as you'll come to regard those plans as just as valid as the time you spend with others. Otherwise, it can be tempting to pass up unspecified me-time in favour of a last-minute invitation somewhere. Through making a plan, particularly a detailed one, you have something that you want to honour. You feel more protective of your alone time, and less likely to pass it up at the drop of a hat for something you don't really want to do with someone else (how many times have you regretted saying you were 'free on Sunday' before being roped into an impromptu get-together with friends-of-friends you've never really liked?). On a practical level, having something concrete in the diary also makes you feel more justified in refusing other activities, because simply put, you've got plans.

A side note: it *can* warrant the occasional raised eyebrow if people ask about your plans and you tell them you'll be spending time alone. That's totally understandable in a world where we don't tend to prioritise alone time in the same way we celebrate togetherness, and it can sometimes mean that friends take it personally. But remember that some of that's in your head, too: we may not publicly acknowledge our need for alonement enough, but that doesn't mean people won't relate to it once you do. From experience, I've been pleasantly surprised by how much people have respected my choice if, for instance, I've planned to have a quiet couple of nights at the beginning of the week. More often than not, they will tell me that sounds like a great idea – and sometimes they will follow suit. Obviously, I have the privilege of, er, my friends knowing that I run a whole platform celebrating alone time, but it's still been a gamechanger to have the vocabulary (i.e., the word alonement) and the confidence to express my need for it.

Avoiding the 'only me' trap

Planning ahead helps us to avoid falling into the 'it's only me' trap, where we practise some bizarre self-flagellation in solitude. Here's what I mean by Only Me-ism:

'Oh, it's only me tonight, so I'll have cereal for dinner.'

'Oh, it's only me, so it doesn't matter if the house is a state.'

'Oh, it's only me, so there's no point buying flowers.'

Don't get me wrong, tidying up for the sake of someone else is considerate. If you love to cook, it's a great joy to invite people round to break bread with. And it's always a lovely gesture to buy someone flowers. But it's problematic if you never show yourself the same kindness. As I'll discuss in Chapter 4, self-care is about simple gestures and comforts; it's about properly meeting your basic needs. You wouldn't expect your partner or close friends to make do with a nutritionally devoid toast and jam 'dinner', so why should *you*, just because you're alone? Alone time isn't an opportunity to deny yourself basic pleasures, as though you're punishing yourself for not having anyone else around. Treating your time alone – however frequent or infrequent – as special is a power move. Holding yourself to the same standards you might in the presence of others sends a message to yourself that you are important. That you have more regard for yourself than the electrician you hastily hoovered the house for. You're not 'only me'. You matter.

Despite this, it's all too easy to fall into a trap of thinking it's only worth making an effort if other people are involved. Radio presenter Vick Hope touched upon this on my Alonement podcast. A fellow live-aloner, she shared that she'd fallen out of the habit of cooking for herself when her relationship ended three years ago, aside from when she hosted friends for dinner. 'I got into a rhythm of not cooking so much; whatever's in the kitchen or whatever's in the fridge I'd just have for dinner or I'd just eat out or I'd get a Deliveroo because I don't really need to be making a big meal for just myself,' she said. However, lockdown caused her to find joy in cooking for herself: 'I found it to be a creative pursuit as well as something that separates my daytime from my night-time' – and to connect with her Nigerian heritage, learning to cook the hearty dishes she'd grown up eating, like jollof rice, okra soup and oxtail stew.

We should be wary of Only Me-ism when planning our 'solitude dates', too. They may not include other people, but that does not mean they need to be low key. You've likely spent a lot of time in your life planning elaborate things to do with friends and families, but has it ever occurred to you to pay yourself the same service? To echo another one of my podcast guests, food writer Felicity Cloake (who also lives alone): You, alone, are worth cooking something nice for. As a partner or a parent, we sometimes harbour an intense shame around planning something special for ourselves, so it's only when we are unexpectedly by ourselves or away for work that we end up discovering this joy. I'm staunchly against this Only Me-ism, which compels us to think time spent alone should be conducted with the modest offerings of an ascetic monk. It creates a basically negative reinforcement situation where time alone = bad, punishing; time with others = redeeming. This is the kind of philosophy that stops us from respecting and valuing alone time. We end up internalising the (destructive) idea that showing love to ourselves is a wasted effort, in the absence of another human. Wrong – it's showing love to the most important person in your world. And on that note . . .

Be utterly selfish (embrace your 'you-ness')

Practising some positive selfishness is no bad thing, and solo dates are a great opportunity to do that. There are so many areas in our lives when we have no choice but to compromise because we have an obligation – as a partner, as an employee, as a parent or as a carer. As one half of a couple, it becomes almost your default setting to shrink your own needs to fit in with a partner's. Your face falls on a first date because the woman opposite you – who you think might be The One – hates cycling, and it's your favourite hobby. You might be looking forward to seeing Emma Stone star in *Cruella*, but accept you might miss it on the big screen because there's no way you could drag your partner along (don't worry, I'll get into that in Chapter 6). I'm not faulting compromise – it's what it takes to make friendships, relationships and families work. What I do take issue with is compromise-by-default; the compromises you don't even know that you're making because you're so used to accommodating someone else. Over time, you forget to know what you wanted in the first place, until you don't even know whether you prefer crunchy or smooth peanut butter.

When socialising with a group of other people, we usually accept that there will be some degree of compromise, even though it can involve solving the complex puzzle of finding a table for five in a central location at a restaurant with a Trip-Advisor rating of 4.5+, all the while factoring in Gemma's late work finish, Jason's strict adhesion to kashrut, the possibility that Sanjay and Grace might bring their baby (or, more likely, will drop out at the last minute) and, last but not least, Sinead's flexi-veganism. Meeting up with other people always involves some level of doing what you don't want to do, even if that's travelling somewhere less-than-convenient or sharing dessert. The pressure associated with suiting the needs of lots of different people – however easygoing and accommodating everyone is – can mitigate the joy of the thing itself, and in the process you compromise-by-default, becoming ever estranged from what you want.

That's where the bliss of selfish solitude comes in. Alone time is a brilliant opportunity to do exactly what you want, without the demands of someone else. There are no moving parts, no other people's chaos. It's all about you. And while this is technically 'selfish', it's also harmless – a positive selfishness, if you will. My podcast guest Daisy Buchanan, who has been married for five years, has long exercised positive selfishness by taking herself out for lunch, which fulfils her desire to be able to sit and enjoy a restaurant meal in relative silence, with a good book. That's why she'll consciously choose a slightly off-peak (and anti-social) time, such as 4pm. She told me: 'I love quiet. I get increasingly overwhelmed by noise, so being able to control the sounds around me appeals.' Doing something that meets your own criteria is a positive assertion that your needs matter – and meeting your own needs ultimately benefits other people, as you are more ready to compromise for others once your needs have already been met – by yourself.

Hazel, 43, celebrated her milestone 40th birthday by taking a solo trip to Whitby, a seaside town in Yorkshire, leaving her two young children back home with her husband. She says she 'thought long and hard' about what she really loved doing and pulled out all the stops: 'I booked myself into my favourite hotel and enjoyed the long scenic train journey there, reading and taking photographs along the way. I took a huge book of John Steinbeck letters, my favourite foods (really fancy olives and chocolates), and when I got there my friend Alison had (as a surprise) ordered champagne to be sent to my room. I also ate lots of fish and chips and went on a boat trip along the coast. It was bloody brilliant.'

Similarly, Clare, 36, takes an annual solo holiday to satisfy whatever her heart desires: a spa afternoon, shopping, eating cheese in a Tuscan piazza. She says: 'I'm a people-pleaser, and my job has always involved keeping other people happy. I've also thrown myself into relationships, because I fully want to find that perfect guy, and have the marriage, and the house, and all that stuff. That's all great, but it can be quite tiring, in a way, so solo travel is my own bit of independence – a time to be absolutely selfish.'

Lockdown proved a perfect time for many people to try 'positive selfishness' out. Commuting and socialising were largely taken off the table – leaving more opportunities for 'me-time' – while, at the same time, many found themselves more conscious of the need for personal space in a shared home. My friend Anna, struggling with an abrupt move from her flat in Peckham to her family home in northern Ireland, found time to herself through working out alone in her bedroom (no gym timetable necessary), while others took solace in daily bubble baths, went off-grid for a while to enjoy box sets or took up a niche hobby (one friend spent weeks absorbed in making wonky-boobed busts out of clay).

Indulging your own selfishness is a straightforward way of practising alonement, because it allows you to take joy in following those personal curiosities and desires, whether that's lingering in the IKEA plant section for 45 minutes or making your fajitas-for-one exactly as spicy as you want, with no apologies. And once you do that a few times, it's likely that it will snowball into even more healthy, positive alone time that you look forward to again and again.

Communicating your alonement needs to others

As touched upon earlier, a regular obstacle to alonement is that it can be taken the wrong way by others; I understand this, because for most of my life, I was the one taking it the wrong way. Introverts make up half of my immediate family. As a teenager, I'd bound down the stairs first thing in the morning looking for someone to talk to, only to enter into what felt like the oppressive silence of my mother and brother – the introvert contingent – doing their morning vigil over crosswords and coffee. It is no exaggeration when I say learning about introversion – and respecting my family members' need for quiet time – radically improved our relationship and brought us closer.

More often than not, the need for alone time stems from totally benign, personal reasons that have nothing to do with the person you're desperately trying not to offend. Yet, time and time again, we find it so hard to communicate our needs to those around us, and this can escalate. You might end up denying yourself alonement altogether or communicating your needs in an awkward way that doesn't come across how you wanted it. So, what's going wrong? It comes down to what I've already talked about: our collective blindspot around the need for solitude. I dare say lockdown moved our understanding along somewhat, as our collective need for space in shared households – with everyone at home at once – became a large part of the global discourse.

The reality, if you're still struggling with this conversation, is that there is no quick fix – but adopting a longer-term commitment to normalising alonement within your relationships or domestic set-up will start to help other people understand and to appreciate it for themselves, too. If all else fails, you could always gift them a copy of this book. Anticipating ways to meet your alonement needs in certain situations so it's not misinterpreted in the moment also helps; for instance, when you're planning a holiday itinerary, communicate that you'd like to have an hour to yourself each day, or make designated space for yourself to be alone in a shared home (more on this in Chapter 10). These conversations may be hard at first, but they will avoid a whole lot of walking on eggshells later on. Once you learn to communicate your needs, quality time spent in your own company is an infinitely positive way to develop your relationship with yourself.

In order to celebrate solitude skills, I crowd-sourced some more examples of how people like to practise their alonement:

'I love going to the gym alone. I set aside time that's totally for myself, and only benefiting myself, and don't feel guilty about it. I can listen to music, do some exercise and – best of all – do some good thinking. If I have a problem in my life, I usually think of the solution while at the gym.' Victoria, 28

'I like to get up at 5.30am while everyone is still asleep and do 45 minutes of yoga. Then, I spend contemplative time preparing a healthy breakfast which I eat on my own in peace and quiet while doing *The Times* crossword. This sets me up for whatever the day throws at me.' Bea, 57

'Bingeing on *Queer Eye* while eating Pump Street Chocolate and drinking Pedro Ximénez sherry wine (because I'm an old lady).' Kat, 27

'My favourite activity to do alone is outdoor cooking. Sitting by an open fire watching my meal change from ingredients to food brings me joy in creating something, it boosts my mood in the calm environment and allows me time to think and set my mind in order.' Alex, 30

'I love buying myself a book from an independent bookshop and reading in bed for an entire evening.' Kara, 29

'Walking with my music blasting. Whether I'm feeling sad, emotional, pensive or happy, it absolutely transports me and takes over in the best way. I feel like I can process things so much better when I'm in this head space.' Liana, 28

'Swimming – anywhere, in the sea, in the pond, in a swimming pool. That's the only time I literally can't distract myself. The monotony of the tiles, sounds, colours, water, the lengths. There is so much clarity to my thoughts whilst I swim: I'm ambitious, I'm creative, I'm fluent in thought in a way I rarely ever am – the minute I get out they immediately cloud.' Amy, 28

'Painting or writing with Classic FM in the background.' Vivien, 67

'Rambling through the woodland parts of Hampstead Heath on puppy-watch, with a large oat milk cappuccino in tow and my phone left at home.' Me, 29

Three easy solitude skills to enhance your alone time

1. Stay away from social media. This will only invalidate the time you're giving to yourself and make you feel FOMO, like everyone's having a better time than you (spoiler – if they're Instagramming in real time, it's likely they're not).

2. Do activities that make you feel good about yourself. Whether that's going for a run to your favourite playlist or taking time to moisturise your entire body, solo time is a great opportunity to work on *you* with self-esteem-boosting activities.

3. Set up some rituals. We're creatures of routine, and there's something comforting in doing the same things regularly. For me, on Saturday mornings I get up early, go to the same local café and read the newspaper. I genuinely look forward to it and value it, and the weekend feels out-of-kilter without it.

The list of solitude skills isn't exhaustive, but the ones I've outlined in this chapter will help you on your way. Depending on your life situation, there are likely many situation-specific ones which need to be brought in; for instance, working out how to balance alonement 'me-time' with 'we-time' if you're in a relationship, or retreating into your inner alonement in the physical presence of young children (Konnie Huq, I applaud you for this). But what's important, I think, is that you consider what proactive steps you need to take to make alone time a positive experience, and one you want to repeat. Talk to your friends and family about it and trade tips. As we've established, alonement is a need for everyone (not just introverts), so the more you can sustain one another's alonement needs, the better. Even if turning alone time into alonement doesn't come naturally, it's something you can work on with the right solitude skills – and believe me, it's more than worth the effort.

4

SELF-CARE

'We must cultivate our own garden.'

(Voltaire)

What my flat lacks in other humans, it more than makes up for in potted plants. You shouldn't have favourites, but I do: a large peace lily from IKEA which perches on a white Marius stool in a corner. It requires very little in order to thrive: watering every few days, indirect sunshine, occasional fertiliser if I'm feeling green-fingered. These basic elements, delivered in the right amounts, combine as if by alchemy; my dependant transforming under my watchful gaze into a verdant, glossy-leaved display, its branches reaching up towards the ceiling. Yet – if I, say, take a weekend city break, and neglect it for a few days, it plays dead – wilting to the floor like a pantomime dame.

My melodramatic potted plant serves as a reminder that I need looking after, too; and I need more than sunshine and water. Alonement, to throw in yet another botanical metaphor, is fertile soil for identifying and looking after your own needs, allowing you to thrive rather than merely survive. This is true whether or not you live with others. Alonement is vital to an authentic, fundamental self-care that sustains you – as an individual with unique needs – in your everyday life.

Always relying on someone else to *take care of you* just doesn't cut it (however compelling Drake and Rihanna made it sound in 2011), because we alone have the most potential to identify and meet our needs. 'I see self-care as self-responsibility,' says Suzy Reading, psychologist and author of *Self-Care for Tough Times*, during an interview for the book. 'That's not to say we don't need other people, but we shouldn't rely solely on others to take care of us. When we learn to get quiet and listen to our bodies, we know ourselves best – it is a skill we develop with practice.'

So, how do we begin?

The origins of self-care

By another name, self-care is just looking after yourself. It's a concept I've discussed at length with my podcast guests, as well as with the wider Alonement community. You're forgiven if the term itself generates a collective eye roll, associating it, as one might, with 28.7 million tagged posts on Instagram and the $4.2 trillion global wellness market.* Self-care has been commodified by capitalism and hijacked by a hashtag, most recognisable in the form of images of freshly baked banana bread (guilty) or bath tubs with a £197 Goop towel set draped over the side. During the 2010s, self-care went from strength to strength as a social media and branding phenomenon; so much so that marketing agency Mintel deemed this period 'the decade that "self-care" went mainstream'.† But its roots are less well known.

Self-care, when you strip it back, has unequivocally unglamorous origins. It can be traced back to the 1950s, long before it was adopted by the wellness movement, when it was used in a medical context. It referred to the practices that institutionalised patients, usually the mentally ill or elderly, were capable of doing to care for themselves, like exercising or administering their own medication without the help of carers.‡ Self-care very much remains 'what it says on the tin' in the medical world. As nurses will know, 'self-care' forms part

---

* Global Wellness Institute, *2018 Global Wellness Economy Monitor*. https://globalwellnessinstitute.org/industry-research/2018-global-wellness-economy-monitor

† Diana Kelter, 'The evolution of self-care', *Mintel*, blog, 23 January 2020. https://www.mintel.com/blog/personal-care-market-news/the-evolution-of-self-care

‡ Aisha Harris, 'A History of Self-Care', *Slate*, 5 April 2017. http://www.slate.com/articles/arts/culturebox/2017/04/the_history_of_self_care.html

of an inpatient's assessment paperwork, yet outside of the hospital ward its meaning has become diluted. A quick Google of the NHS's annual Self-Care Week in November brings up an admittedly rather ugly-looking green and orange PDF outlining the awareness week's key messages, including 'Don't work through your lunch break – look after your health', 'Move more – live well!' and 'Make self-care a lifelong habit'.

Moving more and taking a lunch break might seem like 'florals-for-spring' levels of groundbreaking, particularly if you're used to seeing self-care presented in a more aesthetically pleasing way: a calligraphed Gandhi quote on Instagram, or a monochrome Equinox campaign billboard. But can we learn something from the original no-frills-and-bows approach to self-care?

Misunderstanding self-care

I ask this as a one-time fully paid-up subscriber to the #selfcare movement. I first came across the term in my early twenties, no doubt via my Instagram feed. Entranced by the glamorous image of self-care, I once transformed our shared student bathroom into a crime scene after toppling over a glass of red wine I'd left on the rim of the bathtub. My housemate had to unpick the lock in order to come to my rescue – think damsel in distress meets Gollum, strands plastered to my head by my DIY avocado hair mask, my Lush bath bomb lying unused on the bamboo caddy I'd ordered off Amazon to complete the aesthetic – and sweep up the broken glass from the tiles and burgundy-stained grouting (to prevent me cutting my bare feet) while I observed, naked and useless. The irony of this story? I actually hate baths.

I'm sure I'm not the only one who has unsuccessfully prostrated myself at the high altar of performative self-care. It's become a lucrative buzzword in the cosmetics industry, attached to everything from bath salts to face masks and retinol cream. It can be hard to separate the idea of 'making yourself beautiful' or 'pampering' from 'looking after yourself', suggests Roz, 44. 'I think the beauty industry has co-opted self-care to push the message that if you don't beautify yourself, you don't care about yourself, which is pretty vicious. I feel that we've been fed so many messages about our looks holding our value, that self-care is "pointless" unless it involves some element of beautifying.' She adds: 'I worry that some people will be doing the beauty bits of self-care and not feeling any different afterwards and then beat themselves for doing it "wrong". Which goes completely against the idea of self-care in the first place.'

She has a point. Sometimes, so-called 'me-time' spent pampering feels like something akin to medieval torture. Personally, there is nothing I find less relaxing than fake-tanning: performing a series of gymnastic exercises to apply St. Moritz to my back before standing, frozen like an ill-fated citizen of Pompeii, waiting for my Bisto-coloured, goose-pimpled flesh to dry. You have to credit the beauty industry – and, on a larger level, the patriarchy – for selling us this con. In the past, I've questioned myself for not really enjoying pampering in the way I felt I should do. Yet, when I discussed this with a friend, she said that fake-tanning her legs is a legitimate part of her self-care routine because it improves her confidence. So, er, how do you distinguish between self-care and being a slave to beauty standards?

For Roz, 'The intention is key. If you think doing an expensive sheet mask for 10 minutes while checking your phone or watching TV is going to leave you feeling calm and relaxed, it won't. But doing the same mask with the intention that it's time to look after yourself, switch off from the outside world and listen to some music or use a mindfulness app like Calm, then you'll feel very different.' As long as the 'why' is there, Roz is happy to think of pampering as self-care. 'I love a bubble bath, but if I'm lying there worrying about work or money, that's not self-care. But running a bath and telling myself that the time I'm in it is just for me, I'll deal with everything else when I'm out and there's nothing wrong with shutting out the world for half an hour, *is* self-care.'

Looking back, my so-called 'self-care' was totally mis-guided, especially when considered in relation to my actual university lifestyle: I slept badly, and often, when I did, it was in my make-up, wearing shabby, unwashed pyjamas in fortnight-old sheets. And – importantly – I spent hardly any time alone, save for the hours I spent trying to bake

Deliciously Ella's sweet potato brownies while jamming the NutriBullet (before posting the result on Instagram to all of my 73 followers). The irony of *that* story? I hate baking, too. I wasn't the only person treating self-care as a trend. I shared this with my friend Amy, 28, who had a similar experience. 'Self-care was just something fashionable to do. I'd do a face mask every week religiously, or take a bubble bath every Sunday, and then think: "OK, self-care done, box ticked." It was a task to get done,' she shares.

OK, so Amy and I might both have been technically 'alone' when practising this cookie-cutter version of 'self-care' – but this wasn't alone*ment*. What we thought of as self-care was built on a flimsy premise. The motivation behind it was to serve the Instagram gods, not our own individual needs.

I may not be on board with the fake tan or the baths, but there's one aspect of pampering that is a resoundingly important kind of self-care for me, and that's my skincare regime. Having suffered from an onset of adult acne shortly after starting my first job, I realised how much my mood and self-esteem could be affected by cystic spots and scarring. Since then, my six-step skincare ritual has taken on an almost religious significance in my life; a valid form of self-care and, in its mindful, rhythmic practice, all-important alonement time. Ultimately, what matters is not what you do during your self-care but that it's authentic to you – and ensuring this requires some hard work, offline, first.

Let's go back to basics.

Self-care in the time of coronavirus

Last year, my self-care regime transformed. After a year and a half of living alone, I thought I already knew how to care for myself. At this point, I'd traded baking and baths for digital detoxes and healthy, home-cooked meals (that I ate while they were hot, rather than letting them grow cold while I took share-worthy photos). But my understanding of self-care deepened still when I caught coronavirus at the beginning of March 2020 and had to quarantine alone. In many respects, I was lucky: my case was fairly mild, and my flu-like symptoms eased within a few days (although my sense of smell has still not *quite* recovered). Yet the prospect of being isolated during that unsettling time – without a change of scene or the ability to see anyone else – terrified me, despite being a veteran live-aloner. My fear of not coping drove me to think more meaningfully than ever about what 'proper' self-care constituted, and how I could practise it, proactively, within the four walls of my flat.

I became cut-throat about it, as if I was in a sort of self-care survival mode. Once my health began to improve, I began the days dancing around my bedroom, doing workouts, journalling and ramping up my moisturising regime. My fear of not coping meant I learnt, more radically than ever, to be a friend to myself. I was far from the only person on a self-care crash course; online searches for 'self-care' rose to an all-time high at the end of March 2020 as we entered lockdown, doubling from the beginning of the month.* In the midst of a worldwide pandemic, some of our highest search terms included 'self-care quotes', 'self-care ideas', 'self-care tips' and 'self-care Sunday', which is hardly surprising, if you think about it. Almost everyone experienced some level of upheaval during lockdown, whether that was working from home, being surrounded by young children, being furloughed or made redundant. There was disappointment and grief: weddings were postponed, property purchases fell through, some suffered the loss of loved ones. There was no guidebook for living through an 'unprecedented' pandemic, and for many it took its toll on their mental and physical health. It was a collective crisis, rather than an individual one – and it called, collectively, for greater self-care in order to cope with it.

Lockdown meant that self-care stopped being just a hashtag or a marketing buzzword and started being some-thing we were actively incorporating into our lives. It helped that many of the usual distractions were off the cards. The high street shut its doors; hairdressers and beauticians were closed; Happy Hour was cancelled for the foreseeable future. 'If you look at what people would normally do to care for themselves, it's going out for dinner, having a coffee with

---

* Google Trends, https://trends.google.co.uk/trends/explore?date=today%205-y&geo=GB&q=self%20care

friends, going shopping, all of those things became unavailable to us,' says Reading.

With everyone confined to their homes, life had a strong Groundhog Day feel. Every day felt the same, like you were being tasked to fold up the same sheet of paper in myriad ways. Same lifestyle, same resources, same cast of characters (or solitude if you were living alone) – what would you do with it? Reading believes this time caused a 'seismic shift' in the way self-care was regarded. Once, it was indulgent pampering, but increasingly it became more about 'nourishing practices'. 'It meant finding a new self-care toolkit and embracing self-care in a more holistic way,' says Reading.

I spoke to Amy about this. Before lockdown, she suffered from severe stress and insomnia, which her bubble baths and face masks hadn't improved. 'I had a lot of anxiety about my career, and about how much I had or hadn't achieved before reaching 30 next year.' Her busy life was, in part, a coping mechanism to escape those feelings. 'I was so keen to get out of my head every minute of every day, I needed to be doing something somewhere else: out with friends, seeing my parents' – but then lockdown came around. It forced Amy to slow down and focus on the things that make her happy. She began to prioritise her health and noticed how making simple changes – like taking magnesium after eating and starting the day with a vitamin C tablet – transformed her energy levels during the day, improved her sleep quality and immunity. She adds: 'Over the first three months of lockdown, I completely re-evaluated my priorities, reckoning with how I was really feeling mentally and physically. Self-care went beyond a bath and a face mask to something fundamental.'

Sure, some brands still capitalised on self-care offered up as a commodified panacea – Hommebody, an LA-based loungewear brand endorsed by Emily Ratajkowski, began selling $140 (£110) hoodies tenuously marketed around 'self-care', while Herbivore launched an £87 'self-care essentials' set – but a less glossy and more 'real' kind of self-care also emerged. Yet Andrea Wroble, a health and wellness analyst at Mintel, wrote about how the concept of personal wellness had evolved:* 'Simple ways to incorporate wellness from the comfort of the home or nearby outdoor spaces have taken over as essential practices to maintain connections, release new-found stress and recuperate some semblance of normalcy.'

As I soon discovered, self-care, as it was originally intended, is far less sexy than its Insta-worthy evolution might suggest. The more I reflected on the actual role of self-care in my life, and that of others, the more I saw the value of separating the hashtag from reality.

---

* Andrea Wroble, 'The "next normal" of Covid-19 amplifies basic wellness needs', *Mintel*, blog, 10 June 2020. https://www.mintel.com/blog/personal-care-market-news/the-next-normal-of-covid-19-amplifies-basic-wellness-needs

Caring for the you of tomorrow

Self-care isn't solely about what feels good in the moment. Sure, going for a lunchtime stroll in the sunshine or being snug in bed both feel good, but self-care also takes into account the person you want to be tomorrow. 'Self-care nurtures you in this moment and lovingly tends to the person you're becoming,' says Reading. 'Sometimes, that can mean delayed gratification.' After all, self-care, at the heart of it, isn't about coping at your minimum possible capacity. It's about creating a foundation of yourself that can help you thrive, asking yourself who it is that you want to grow into, and how can you nurture that dream. I think about this in terms of Maslow's hierarchy of needs theory. For the uninitiated, twentieth-century American psychologist Abraham Maslow famously depicted a human's 'hierarchy of needs' in a pyramid model. The theory is through fulfilling basic physiological needs – like sleep, food and sex – you are able to progress towards meeting the higher ones.

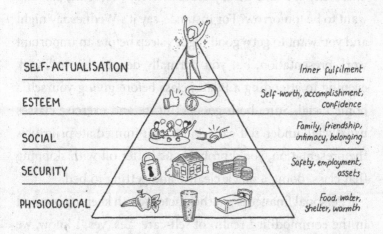

SELF-ACTUALISATION — Inner fulfilment

ESTEEM — Self-worth, accomplishment, confidence

SOCIAL — Family, friendship, intimacy, belonging

SECURITY — Safety, employment, assets

PHYSIOLOGICAL — Food, water, shelter, warmth

Self-care facilitates a space to meet those lower, fundamental needs, such as eating well, getting enough sleep and fulfilling your sexual needs through masturbation or with a partner. These then become building blocks that provide the basis for self-esteem (feeling good about yourself) and self-actualisation. When it comes to self-esteem, self-care is essential because it sends a message to yourself, regularly, that you matter enough to do these things for. You are *enough* to run a whole hot bath for – yes, just for you. As for the intense-sounding self-actualisation part – finding the thing that makes your individual life, alone, feel meaningful is a key part of alonement (more on this in the next chapter), so any practices that sustain this are important.

Nowadays, whenever I find myself over-complicating my self-care, I like to strip it back by thinking about Maslow's 'hierarchy of needs' theory. Does this *really* serve the person I want to be tomorrow? For instance, say it's Wednesday night and you want to get a good night's sleep before an important work presentation, but you normally devote this midweek evening to attending a Pilates class before giving yourself a home facial. Sure, both good skincare and exercise classes usually fall under 'self-care', but if your immediate priority is the presentation, you'd probably be better off with skipping that class, doing a quick cleanse and getting to bed.

Personal finance is another factor worth keeping in mind in the commodified realm of self-care. Yes, yes, I know, we all like to say, 'Fuck it, treat yo'self', but sometimes it can be a self-care move to *not* buy that £47 Diptyque candle if splurging will have negative knock-on effects. 'Sorting finances out and gaining control is the ultimate self-care for me,' says Hayley, 27, who is currently saving to buy a house with her partner. 'If you actually buy all the things you're told you "need" for self-care, you end up wasting money which then stresses you out, causing panic and fear around money.'

As I discussed earlier, we are constantly overstimulated by the background noise of so many voices competing for attention against our own – and this is particularly true of something as marketable as self-care. In order to keep your self-care true to you, you need to remember what *you* want.

The Boring Parent theory

Much of self-care, once you strip it back, is unsexy and unglamorous yet, sometimes in equal measure, transformational. In reality, most of the things that actually constitute self-care are unlikely to feature on your Instagram feed. For instance, I have chronically dry skin so I use an aqueous face cream from a brand called Eucerin, which contains an ingredient called urea, a component of – you guessed it – urine (although I'm assured only synthetic versions are used in cosmetics). I'm going to be honest, I won't be chronicling my Eucerin habit on my grid anytime soon, but it serves something much greater than Instagram: me. In truth, many of our behind-closed-doors self-care practices *aren't* sexy, but the results are.

Other 'unsexy' versions of self-care (some crowd-sourced among my friends) can include:

- A baked potato
- An early bedtime
- Flossing
- Those exfoliating foot gloves
- Giving yourself a scalp massage
- Taking a nap
- Putting your phone on Airplane mode
- Folding laundry

- Taking three deep breaths
- Making a cup of tea
- Cutting your toenails
- Eating Hobnobs
- Going to the dentist
- Doing the washing up

Still, it's easy to get waylaid, and I often do if I get a sponsored advert for White Company cashmere socks or come across a jazzy-looking Ottolenghi recipe on Twitter. Sometimes, when I find myself overcomplicating self-care, or losing track of why I'm doing what I'm doing, I try to imagine an extremely boring, reliable parent figure and I become that person to myself.

Let me introduce you to the Boring Parent. This isn't a mocktail-wielding Cool Mom à la *Mean Girls*. This is the 'square' parent who washes your PE kit on time, makes sure you brush your teeth and shows an almost religious zeal for early bedtimes. It's the reliable parent who picks you up from the party at 9pm in their Toyota Prius, abiding by the 30mph speed limit all the way home with Radio 4 playing softly in the background. Sometimes, the Boring Parent is a total killjoy, because they know that, unless your basic needs are fulfilled, you won't be able to meet the more complex ones (as anyone who has ever tried to get through a working day after bingeing *Killing Eve* all night will know). This is why I try to channel my inner Boring Parent – so that I can achieve the self-actualisation at the top of Maslow's pyramid. For instance, during a week where I have a lot of deadlines and limited time to complete them, I'll have to concede to my inner Boring Parent when it points out that, actually, meeting a friend for an Aperol Spritz (which will likely spiral into two or three) isn't the best idea. I have to admit to myself that, while it might feel relaxing in the short term, it will leave me with a mental fog that will make me feel slower the next day, creating a cycle of guilt and panic.

Caring for yourself as an adult is a lot more complicated than caring for a child, because it isn't a 'one-size-fits-all' policy. It's not as straightforward as 'eat your greens' and an early bedtime; figuring out what works for you from a self-care perspective can be the work of a lifetime. Should you be laying off caffeine after midday? Should you eat dairy? Is a HIIT class straight after work a brilliant way to relieve stress, or does dreading it all day counteract the effects? Do you *need* to meditate?

The rules are there are no rules, but it helps to have parameters and to let the Boring Parent have a look in to make sure your self-care mission meets its purpose. Effective self-care should be underpinned by a concern for your most basic needs – air, food, water, shelter – and motivated by your own, more individual, higher ones. Case in point: online searches about self-care tend to peak between 11pm and 3am. You know what would be a really good form of self-care? Not being online at 2am Googling 'self-care'. Thanks for the tip, Boring Parent. Tuning in to a yoga video online is an excellent good way to look after your body and create a sense of mental harmony, but you need to remember to focus on your breathing – not just whether you'll ever perfect a tree pose or get the instructor's toned upper arms. Cheers, Boring Parent-turned-Yogi.

However you rationalise it, it's important to stop thinking of 'self-care' as something that's aesthetically pleasing, and to remind yourself of the beyond-exciting, brilliant, self-actualised future version of you that it's serving (spoiler alert: this is a never-ending journey, but it's a worthy one). For my friend Tam, 32, self-care means removing as many complications as possible from his life. For context, Tam is an ambitious registrar doctor who goes for 10km runs at the end of his night shifts. It's exhausting even to write about, but undeniably impressive. So, I was intrigued – if a little surprised – to learn of his self-proclaimed 'boring' self-care routine. Tam explained that during weeks where he anticipates he might be stressed – for instance when working a series of night shifts – he'll reduce other potential stressors from his life. 'I'll sometimes eat the same nutritionally balanced meal four or five times a week, like a Waitrose prepared quinoa salad with cottage cheese and tomatoes, and I have ten of the same shirts from Charles Tyrwhitt in seven different colours.' Living in a self-inflicted Groundhog Day throughout the working week might not suit everyone, but, for Tam, it's a form of emotional and physical self-care; this finely tuned schedule allows him to remove stress from his personal life while making sure he's still nourishing his body, freeing up mental energy to help him thrive at work.

I spoke to personal trainer and author Alice Liveing on my Alonement podcast, who boasts hundreds of thousands of Instagram followers and a series of lucrative endorsement deals. Despite Alice's own glossy brand, her attitude towards self-care is refreshingly simple. She said: 'Sometimes self-care can be getting out of bed in the morning or having a shower. What we've done is glamorise self-care when it can really be the mundane things that are the most caring acts we can do for ourselves. Cooking a nice dinner or turning off your laptop at 6pm instead of working into the evening. We need to lose the idea that self-care looks a certain way – that you can succeed or fail at it.'

The real self-care pioneers

Here's a revelation that would have surprised my 21-year-old self in the lukewarm bathtub: the best self-care pioneers are *not* the influencers posting to their 300k+ followers about their quartz facial rollers. Those who take their own self-care most seriously are, without a fail, those who have experienced the adverse effects when self-care goes out the window. 'Self-care is health care; it's not until your health is genuinely impinged that you realise this,' says Reading.

When I interviewed Jonny Benjamin on the podcast, he spoke about how, when he was in his early 20s, he was hospitalised and later diagnosed with schizoaffective disorder. Despite being on suicide watch, Jonny escaped from the psychiatric hospital where he was being treated and stood on the edge of Waterloo Bridge, intending to take his own life. A stranger named Neil Laybourn intervened, saving Jonny's life. Jonny, now 33, works full time as a mental health campaigner. What he has learnt, after multiple hospitalisations and therapy, is that self-care, for him, is non-negotiable. He said on the podcast: 'Just like other parts of the body, my brain can become unwell and I've learnt to manage it. You know to ask for help, if you're having a heart attack you don't just think "I'll deal with it tomorrow". There have been periods of time when I've thought I'm going to pretend it's not there but ultimately it makes me worse, so I've got to the point where I'll deal with it there and then.'

Before I spoke to Jonny, I felt that it would be insensitive to ask someone who had suffered what I regarded as *real* trauma – such as, in Jonny's case, a serious mental health disorder – about self-care, something that so often can be perceived as a frivolous marketing buzzword. But, actually, he spoke at length about his love of bubble baths, scented candles and digital detoxes, because he'd identified those things as important for looking after his mental health. Since speaking to Jonny, I've found those with the best understanding of self-care – and the most simple, effective toolkits to practise with – tend to be those who have overcome adversity, rather than the influencer touting the CBD drops. Who knew?

How self-care benefits others

We're beginning to acknowledge that self-care is about more than just us. This idea is presented in an episode of the Netflix series *Never Have I Ever*, where character Ben Gross, a high school student, struggles with his absentee parents. He returns home to find his mother leaving the house with a wheelie suitcase.

'Hey sweetie, no time to talk, I'm going to a self-actualisation retreat in Santa Barbara.'

'Didn't you just do that?'

'No, I went to a mindfulness workshop in Santa Clara. Similar concept, very different philosophies.'

'OK, have fun!'

'It's not fun, Ben. It's work. On me. So I can be a better mom – to you! Gotta run!'

I know – this is a total parody. But it taps into something meaningful: that self-care isn't just for you, but instead, according to Reading, a value that 'affects every realm of your life' allowing you to be, for instance, 'a better parent; a better spouse; a better friend'. As Jonny said on the podcast: 'I never understood the card on the aeroplane that says put your oxygen mask on first – that you need to give yourself the oxygen before you can give it to anyone else. But now I do – and I understand that analogy is the same with real life. I've got to the point in recent years where I've given so much of myself and it can be exhausting, I'd just give, give, give, but through therapy I've realised that I need to give to myself as well.'

Learning to look after yourself – to identify and meet your own needs – will reap benefits for those around you. Not only will you be better placed to take care of others, but you will be able to give valuable cues to the people in your life about how they might show care or love to you, rather than taking a stab in the dark.

Putting the 'self' in self-care

After interviewing Jonny, it struck me as wrong that people often only start taking self-care seriously when they are pushed to the extreme. So many of us live on autopilot because we think we can neglect our needs and nothing bad will happen. All will be forgotten by the time of our next holiday or when we next see our friends at the pub; but self-care isn't just getting by in the moment until the next thing comes along, it's what sustains the best possible version of us day to day. I firmly believe that a pandemic or issues arising from mental health shouldn't be the only things to force us to care for ourselves, so I asked Reading for her best advice for developing your own, personal self-care regime before a crisis strikes. She stressed that self-care needs to be personal to you – something that can be hard to remember when you are constantly bombarded with things pertaining to offer 'self-care' benefits on the internet, like that aforementioned Diptyque candle or 'indulgent' Galaxy chocolate. That's where checking in with yourself and your own individual needs comes in. It's important to ask yourself first: is this for *me*? Or am I simply being targeted on Google Ads as a consequence of the average 24–30-year-old young professional demographic's historic buying habits?

The ability to identify what works for you, offline and outside of the latest trend, is crucial to really caring for yourself – and this starts with, you guessed it, time alone. If you take this alonement time to reflect on your choices and decisions, you learn to observe what's going on in your body and mind and steer clear of unhelpful (and bankruptcy-inducing) distractions.

Self-care MOT

When you start thinking about your own self-care regime, it can be overwhelming. Start by writing down a list of the things that make you feel happy, calm and grounded. These are your self-care priorities. My list looks something like this:

Clean hair

Post-exercise endorphins

Podcasts

Buttered toast

Silence

A new novel

Lindt dark chocolate with sea salt

Being outside

Moisturised skin

Gingham flannel pyjamas

Fresh coffee

Reading a long-form magazine feature

Eating a huge salad full of fresh ingredients

Being in tidy spaces

I've also written down a number of useful questions to ask yourself while you're reflecting on your day-to-day life:

- How soon after waking up do you turn your phone on, and what effect does this have on you?
- How does the food you eat affect your mood?
- How much sleep do you need to thrive, rather than simply to function?
- What makes you feel calm in your immediate surroundings?
- What daily habits are non-negotiable?
- What's the comfiest underwear you own?
- When during the day do you feel calmest?
- When during the day do you feel most stressed?
- Who in your life makes you feel happiest?
- Who makes you feel low every time you see or speak to them?

This list isn't exhaustive, but it's a great starting point for mindfully reflecting on how you spend your time, and what you might tweak in the name of self-care. Once you start practising *real* self-care, you will see the positive benefits it brings to your life and, in turn, start seeking out the alone time to do it.

5

DOING YOUR THING

'What do you do?' It's a question many of us dread, and yet it's usually one of the first ones asked by strangers, hot on the heels of trading first names we'll instantly forget. 'And what do you do?' asks Kate – or was it, Katrina? – thrust in your direction by a harried host, or a bride and groom attempting to say hello to everyone in the room in the 20-minute gap between dinner courses. There's a certain logic to asking this question. Those of us in full-time work will often spend more hours interacting with our colleagues than our own families or friends. When we factor in what we're actually *doing* for most of our lives, working (or sleeping) tends to come in first place.

Some people really like being asked this question (I suspect some only ask it so they can answer it themselves). If I'm honest, I always quite liked saying I was a journalist. Other jobs I imagine are fun to talk about at parties, for various reasons, include:

- A doctor
- A fashion designer
- A restaurant critic
- An astronaut
- Jamie Dornan's body double
- A Pret sandwich taster
- Anyone who works for Google

Then there are those whose identity and creative passion closely aligns with what they do for a living, such as architects, actors and artists – but they're the exception, rather than the rule. For most of us this question makes us inwardly sigh, because it means revealing an industry we're unsure about, a job title we're frustrated with or a well-known corporation that we don't want to be defined by. Some people straight up dodge the question. A friend of mine describes himself as a 'musician' first and foremost, despite the fact that his consultancy role at Deloitte – which he grudgingly refers to as his 'day job' – takes up between 14 and 15 hours of each weekday. Another friend works in PropTech heading up a sales team – a job he loves, incidentally – yet amuses himself by pretending he hasn't understood the 'what do you do?' question. 'Well, Steve, I do a lot of running and listening to podcasts,' he'll respond to a confused interlocutor, not missing a beat.

Let's factor in that 37 per cent of British workers consider their jobs to be completely meaningless. Only half (50 per cent) of those surveyed said they thought their jobs were meaningful, while 13 per cent weren't sure.* Which, all in all, makes the 'what do you do?' question a fairly crap opener. The issue is that what we *do* as our day job is a pretty reductive way to convey who we *are*. Yet, in the twenty-first century, our jobs have come to be seen as 'the crucible of individuality', according to The School of Life's *A Replacement for Religion*: 'When we meet a stranger, we do not, as in the past, ask them about their ancestors, their religion or the place they grew up in. We ask them, first and foremost, what they "do", for it is our work that has, more than anything else, come to be seen as the crucible of our individuality.' To conflate your job with your sense of self might make some sense, particularly given the sheer number of hours we spend working – and days are, to paraphrase Philip Larkin, where we live – but how close does your job title get to revealing who you are as a person? Generally, not very, because, at the end of the day, you work for a business, not a finishing school for self-actualisation.

My cousin Natalie, 32, loves her job as a lawyer in the City, and she's very good at it, but for her, dancing is distinct from her time in the office, because it serves her soul

---

* Will Dahlgreen, '37% of British workers think their jobs are meaningless', *YouGov*, 12 August 2015. https://yougov.co.uk/topics/lifestyle/articles-reports/2015/08/12/british-jobs-meaningless

in a way a City law firm simply can't. 'You get a reward when you are successful, like a pay rise or a bonus, but most of the time you're doing work for other people – it's not solely for you.' Yes, we live in an ambitious society and it's important to get a sense of progression and achievement within your job, but, as Daisy Buchanan said on my Alonement podcast, it's 'dangerously easy . . . to tie achievement to self-worth'. Piling too much pressure on our workplaces to give our lives an ultimate purpose and meaning can often leave us, at best, disappointed, at worst storming out of the Monday morning sales meeting when that existentialist *ennui* gets too much. Natalie describes dancing as the space where 'I can be completely myself – dance is *me*.' She adds: 'I wouldn't live a happy life without dance and music. It allows me to escape the pressures of the world around me.'

Natalie reinforces why it's so important to pursue the things you love, outside of your working life – because, otherwise, how else do you build a sense of personal identity? If we don't devote time to doing the thing, or things, that ignite our souls, we end up being defined either by our jobs or – the other option – who we are in relation to other people and within social institutions. Think back to that party scenario. Unless the person you're talking to has some 'fun and quirky icebreakers' up their sleeve, many classic follow-up questions to 'what do you do?' revolve around your marital status or where you were educated:

Are you single? Do you have children? What school did you go to? What university? More often than not, there's an undertone of implicit judgement about your social status or lifestyle choices, which you might not mind – particularly if you went to a well-known public school, Oxbridge, or happen to have a recently acquired engagement ring on your finger – but it's limiting, too. Even if you have the 'right' answers, how much does that really say about who you are – and where your passion lies?

What don't you do?

Perhaps the *real* reason so many of us hate the 'what do you do' question is because it reminds us so painfully of what we *don't* do in the alone time that we have available to us. Perhaps it simply acknowledges the gulf between how we spend our time and who we really want to be. Do you spend your evenings and weekends scrolling through Instagram and Twitter, or finding yourself on page 17 of the 'Going out-out' section on ASOS, or rewatching *The Only Way is Essex* series 1, or planning a hen do, or monitoring the 'online' WhatsApp status of last week's date who never messaged you back? Or do you spend it doing what you love?

Most of us have *some* degree of leisure time in our lives. There are obvious exceptions to this, such as people working in industries like nursing or banking, or those first years of parenting where, I hear on the grapevine, you might struggle for ten minutes of loo-based alonement. But in general? Most of us have spare time in our days. The average British person spends 29 per cent of their daily leisure time – an average of 100 minutes a day – on their own.* The question is: how do we use it?

What do you do – for you?

Alonement time is the perfect opportunity for exploring a passion or a hobby – effectively, anything that feels life-affirming outside of your work or relationships. Trouble is, time committed to exploring our passion is generally the first thing we let go in the face of external pressures (like, you know, working through our lunch break or going on a promising Tinder date). It's all too tempting to conclude that nebulous things like self-growth and filling your soul don't matter in the face of more nagging professional or social concerns. We've historically had a similar negative bias towards self-care activities, although, as mentioned

---

* According to the Office for National Statistics, leisure time is defined as the time when people are not working (including unpaid work like house-work and caring for family members), studying, commuting or doing basic activities for existence like sleeping and eating at home. https://www.ons.gov. uk/peoplepopulationandcommunity/wellbeing/articles/britsspend29oftheir leisuretimealone/2018-06-22

in the previous chapter, we're starting to understand the importance of prioritising our mental and physical health (you might not quite get away with the ol' 'sorry I'm washing my hair that night' excuse, but tell someone candidly you're burnt out and dying for an early night and they'll understand why you can't come for Friday drinks). Alone time spent 'finding yourself' can be harder to justify, both to ourselves and to other people. It's hard not to feel that a night in working on your oil painting is voluntary and therefore easily changeable in a way that working late or attending a group fajita night isn't. Meanwhile, while it might enrich your soul, it doesn't quite have the same translatable wellbeing benefits as self-care (like an early night or a run) might. *It's just a hobby.*

My friend Siobhan, one of the most accomplished people I know, has encountered this attitude in the past. For context, Siobhan is grade eight on piano, trilingual and has the voice of an angel. Outside of her impressive job at a content marketing agency, she has always had a couple of hobbies on the go: she's been a member of a choir, an orchestra and a tap-dancing troupe. She's also a member of an improvisational comedy group (with whom she performed at the Edinburgh Fringe Festival) and has recently taken up roller derby. We can't all be Siobhan (in all honesty, I have a theory she's actually a set of triplets masquerading as one person, or else she's got one of those Time-Turner devices like Hermione in *Harry Potter*). But what I never fail to admire about her is that she gives time to these activities, creating space in her weekly schedule for her to challenge herself and grow. 'The world is full of interesting things, so it's always seemed like a shame not to try them. Having hobbies and interests has helped me define my own identity; improvisational comedy makes me more confident, creative and decisive, while roller derby has allowed me to learn something new, and I feel proud of myself after seeing a visible improvement.' She has always kept these hobbies up in and out of relationships: 'I've never wanted to be defined by a partner, or to rely on anyone else for my happiness and have them rely on me for theirs.' Yet her outside interests proved a tension during a four-year-long relationship. 'My ex-boyfriend would often make comments that we didn't see each other enough and that we needed to schedule more time together. Rarely would he say it outright, but I definitely felt that he thought I should ditch some of my hobbies to prioritise him. It didn't help that he didn't have any of his own.'

In western culture, we suffer from a habit of dismissing activities that fulfil no social, or financial, or professional purpose, even if those activities are giving your life purpose. We might end up praising the 'overnight success' of someone who has pursued their thing enough to make it profitable, or at least to go viral on social media, but, day to day, we fail to encourage the pursuit of that very 'thing' that might make our individual lives more meaningful and enjoyable. So how, exactly, do we emphasise the importance of our 'thing' to other people? It proved hard to find a precedent in British culture, but I eventually found traction in the Japanese idea of *ikigai*, which refers to having a direction or purpose in life that makes one's life worthwhile, whereas the French have *raison d'être*: literally, a reason for being. What I like about these (relatively similar) concepts is that they don't revolve around your day job; for instance, in a perfect world, someone's ikigai is the convergence of their profession, their passion, what the world needs and where their talents lie, while a person's *raison d'être* – what motivates them in life and gives them a sense of purpose – can be fishing, or painting, or performing stand-up comedy or practising karate. Whether it brings you fame and fortune or not, having a 'thing' that sets your soul alight is intrinsically valuable.

Be honest with yourself: how much time are you giving to the *things* you love? People will say they have a certain hobby – or, at least, it will be represented somewhere on their CV or by the rockclimbing shot on their Hinge profile – except, when you ask them how much time they spend doing it, it's fairly minimal. They like the *idea* of doing this particular thing, or else feel like they should do more of it (keeping up a childhood talent for sketching, perhaps), but, for one reason or another, the actual *doing* of it often falls to the wayside. A personal confession: I've always identified with the romantic notion of being a writer, yet there have been periods of my life – lasting years, in some cases – where I've hardly put pen to paper outside of academic or professional work. I probably saw myself on one level as a 'writer', but I was a fraud to myself, and to my thing.

Yet, I'm lucky in that I found my thing quite early on in life, making up songs and writing stories from the age of six, and deep down, I've always felt a stronger sense of purpose when I'm writing, compared to anything else. Trouble is, once I reached puberty, writing outside of school all-too-often took a backseat to concerns with, well, basically anything else. I was boy-mad, for a start. Quite often I'd fixate on someone I fancied – ironically, many of whom I admired for their own passion, curiosity and drive – and I'd sit daydreaming about them during lessons (Maths, Chemistry and Physics lessons were particularly conducive to these moments of reverie). Later, and for most of my adult life, to be honest, I'd fall asleep thinking about a romantic interest, rather than my own dreams and ambitions, however unworthy the candidate. The less well I knew them, the better. My 'thing' was never a priority because my time and mental energy was all-too-frequently invested in the likes of Zack, 32, from West Hampstead, with whom I'd shared a bottle of Sauvignon Blanc followed by a 7/10 kiss the previous Thursday evening. In short, no romantic dalliance was too inconsequential to distract me from devoting time to my truest and most enduring love: writing. In my two long-term relationships, my time-management wasn't much better; we'd WhatsApp during the day and spend hours on the phone before bed. I'd also – single or otherwise – spend almost all my spare time seeing friends, filling up weekends with back-to-back coffees and brunches and cocktails, not to mention all the time I spent on social media. So, why was I failing to show much love to the thing I love?

The importance of time alone

Practically speaking, the main thing keeping me from doing my thing was that I spent next to no time alone, doing it. But then, that was a conscious decision. It's not like I had many pressing, real-life obligations outside of work; I could definitely afford to socialise less and still have close friends and family, or to have some semblance of a dating life without making Hinge my most time-consuming (pseudo) hobby. Underneath it all, I think my commitment to 'busy-ness' was motivated by fear. Committing to writing meant spending time alone, something I was unfamiliar with. It meant actively carving time out of my week to be with just me. It also meant facing the discomfort of my own thoughts: including, as I mentioned in Chapter 2, that pesky inner critic. Yet, ultimately, in order to achieve my dreams, I had to take a step back from my social-centric lifestyle and face this time alone, overcoming my fears and doubts, investing in myself and honing my skills.

Alonement allows you to invest in your sense of greater purpose and meaning – and, in the process, to build a core of you-ness that isn't defined by what you 'do'. You may pay lip service to the idea of self-growth – liking a #Monday Motivation post on Instagram, watching inspiring Ted Talks about entrepreneurship – but until you make the space in your life for you, it's unlikely to happen. Psychiatrist Anthony Storr agrees. In his book *Solitude*, he wrote that 'human beings easily become alienated from their own deepest needs and feelings. Learning, thinking, innovation and maintaining contact with one's own inner world are all facilitated by solitude.' Maslow was on board: he identified the ability to spend time alone, together with having privacy and autonomy, to be among the qualities of self-actualising people.* For both these experts, time alone is vital for finding and practising your passion.

Lockdown compelled many of us to start taking our hobbies and interests more seriously. Between being furloughed, working from home or forbidden from seeing friends and family, our employment and our social lives were suddenly no longer at the centre of our existence – forcing us to get more inventive with our spare time. Happily, it was during this period that I witnessed so many people around me finding their thing: dressmaking, bullet-journalling, make-up

---

* Rose Cherneva, 'Self-Actualization as a Sign of Personal Development', *Medium*, 9 June 2020. https://medium.com/the-sixth-sense/self-actualization-as-a-sign-of-personal-development-bf21c8037fd

artistry, gardening, roller skating. Chris, 30, took this time out to nurture his passion for DJing, practising alone and then doing virtual sets for his friends over Zoom. 'I enjoy that it's something creative, which in my work I feel is an area of my brain I don't utilise much,' he tells me. 'It's completely different and very therapeutic. I have a lot of ideas in my head the whole time, about songs that might mix well, and trying them out is both great fun and relaxing.' While Chris loves the social element of DJing during performance – both live and virtually – in private it's me-time for him, both to zone out and be fully absorbed, away from other people or his phone. A former music scholar, he loves the sense of satisfaction it gives him as he mixes one song seamlessly into the next.

Doing your thing can often be associated with a psychology term known as 'intrinsic motivation'. In a nutshell, this is when you are driven to do something because the activity alone is personally rewarding, like learning Dutch because you like the way it sounds (as opposed to extrinsic motivation – i.e. learning Dutch because you're relocating to Amsterdam for work). That doesn't mean intrinsic motivation can only happen when you're by yourself; some hobbies by their very nature need to be practised with others, and that's OK; the salient point is that you are doing something motivated by you, for you. Camilla Thurlow learnt the value of intrinsic motivation when she began her job as an explosive ordnance disposal expert. Camilla spent her academic career 'always looking for a way to prove myself to the world around me. I'd do the projects that got me marks and feedback, to look good. It was performative.' Yet, when she began working for The HALO Trust clearing landmines, 'it wasn't about trying to prove anything to anyone anymore, it just had a meaning in itself.'

You may not always be physically alone when you do your thing, but you alone will experience:

- That safe, reassuring feeling that you are exactly where you should be right now
- The goosebumps you get when, for instance, you perfect playing a piece of music, or create something beautiful
- The intense excitement flowing through you when you talk about the 'thing' you're passionate about
- The burst of creativity that comes out of nowhere, throwing up inspiration that never occurred to your conscious brain

Prioritising your thing

You know that person who always says, 'Oh I'd love to do X,' but instead fills up their calendar with back-to-back social activities? *Don't* be that person. Finding your thing is, put simply, a case of allocating time for yourself to find it. Equally, if you have a passion or an interest in something already, you have to dedicate time to pursuing it. You would be hurt if a friend or partner never spent any quality time with you, so don't show this apathy towards your passions, either. OK, so we know it isn't a case of spending a couple of hours alone and suddenly your dreams come true; alonement is the time for you to identify your thing and actively take steps to start doing it. As we've established, time alone is time dedicated to you, and by extension it should be devoted to your thing, too, whether or not you know what it is yet. A good starting point is by daring to make space for it in your life.

On a practical level, getting comfortable with being alone is useful for trying out a new passion. If you don't feel confident enough to, say, enter a room of unfamiliar people by yourself – whether that's a boxing gym or a ballet class – it's likely you will miss out on doing a whole lot of activities that may, potentially, be your thing. My friend Amy, who became hooked on boxing six years ago, considers her twice-weekly group training sessions a 'non-negotiable' (the instructor calls her the most committed member). Carving out 'non-negotiable' alonement time for myself was what got me out of the endless cycle of *feeling* like a writer but not actually doing much writing. Thanks to my New Year's resolution to spend more time alone, I ended up having a lot more time to write outside of my day job on an editorial team. In the Saturday mornings I ring-fenced for myself, in the hours before bed when I switched off my phone, in the weeknights I refused to spend with people I didn't know very well, I found the time to write what morphed into a 100-odd page document of 'random notes' containing the rudiments of this very book.

What if I don't have a thing?

For some, your thing is intuitive. For others, finding what you most enjoy can be a lifelong quest – but one hell of a worthy one. A great place to start is doing what the author Elizabeth Gilbert calls 'creative living'. This isn't specific to being an 'artist' or working in a creative industry; in her book *Big Magic*, Gilbert describes simply 'living a life that is driven more strongly by curiosity than by fear'.

I was reminded of Gilbert's concept of creative living when I spoke to model and activist Jada Sezer, whose sense of curiosity and passion for life was infectious. She had just got her motorcycling licence when I interviewed her for the podcast: 'There's something about riding with the wind in your hair . . . it's incredibly mindful.' She also paints and practises hot yoga – and is committed to the idea of 'giving herself time' to pursue these hobbies and commitments, which she values because they nurture her as an individual. Some other examples of creative living:

- Jigsaw puzzles
- Playing a musical instrument
- Moodboarding
- Dancing
- Reading fiction
- Martial arts
- Gardening
- Knitting or sewing
- Flower arranging
- Coding
- Joining an improv comedy group
- DJing
- Life drawing
- Making jam

Another helpful way to think of your thing is through positive psychologist Mihaly Csikszentmihalyi's concept of 'flow': a state whereby you are fully immersed in a certain task, feeling a sense of enjoyment, focus and energy as you do it. Effectively, this sense of purpose and 'flow' is the easiest way to identify your 'thing': the thing you do just for yourself and are interested in just for itself, that brings you a sense of you-ness that isn't defined by your job or your relationships.

Your thing often reflects who you are as a person, because it's a reflection of not only your strengths, but what motivates you deep inside your soul. I realised this recently during a conversation with my brother. He loves looking at the intricate details of systems and doesn't find individual human psychology particularly interesting, whereas most of what I do requires some sort of human element to keep me motivated. This is why I enjoy spending hours with my girlfriends discussing our feelings over Oyster Bay Sauvignon Blanc, while my brother enjoys single-handedly constructing all of the IKEA flatpack furniture in his flat, teaching himself to play Mozart on the piano and learning conversational Spanish. Or so I tell myself.

In any case, we are all special and unique, and that's part of the reason why it's so important to have a 'thing'; we need to celebrate our uniqueness. What's freeing about this is that it reduces the all-too-common urge to compare ourselves with others, because our 'thing' is motivated by our sense of individuality, not an inferiority complex. Once you start practising your thing, it becomes an important way to define who you are – not in relation to others, but to yourself.

Doing your thing can be life-changing

Your thing won't necessarily be how you spend the bulk of your time, but building time in your routine to 'do you' will have a positive effect on other areas of your life. It may even cause you to live longer: the Japanese island of Okinawa, where the concept of *ikigai* originated, has the largest population of centenarians (people aged 100 or over) in the world.*

Here's how else it will positively impact your life.

Self-growth in other areas

Boxing has helped Amy grow outside of the boxing ring, too, pushing her to overcome a fear of confrontation that had previously impacted both her work and her friendships. 'I think it's made me more confident to communicate with people about how I feel,' she explains. 'There have definitely been times in my life where I've known I'm not happy with something but I've kept it inside me and not mentioned it, because no one's brought it up. But boxing has changed that. It's very black and white, and I feel like that language of directness translates into my everyday life, meaning I find it easier to express what I want. I've also learnt to be more fearless, because if I can get punched in the face, I can tell someone that I don't like something they do. I still hate confrontation but nowadays I think "I'll probably survive it".'

Producing and hosting my podcast – which began as a hobby and is now part of my career – has shown me that I'm

---

* Thomas Oppong, 'Ikigai: The Japanese Secret to a Long and Happy Life Might Just Help You Live a More Fulfilling Life', *Medium*, 10 January 2018. https://medium.com/thrive-global/ikigai-the-japanese-secret-to-a-long-and-happy-life-might-just-help-you-live-a-more-fulfilling-9871d01992b7

a hell of a lot more capable than I ever thought I was. Not only did I develop a whole different technical skillset outside of traditional journalism, but my podcasting journey also taught me a valuable personal skill: to ask for help. Weirdly, taking on a discipline that I'd never had training in and accepting that I was a fairly clueless podcast newbie liberated me to move forward, rather than waste time berating myself for what I didn't know. I'd start every day with a list of Impossible Questions, such as, 'How do you edit out a plosive?' and 'How do you get a podcast on Apple?' and seek out the answers, knowing I, alone, was responsible for finding them out (with thanks to some brilliant mentors and helpers along the way). Over time my self-confidence grew as I recognised how far I had come.

Attracting others

Having a thing can also be attractive to others. I discussed this on my podcast with LBC radio presenter Matthew Stadlen, a keen birdwatcher, who suggested that having a passion can be 'intoxicating'. He said: 'It's intoxicating for others when someone's really excited about something, even if it's something as quirky as birdwatching.' He has a point. About a year ago, I went on a date with a man who dropped into conversation that he'd really gotten into 'hobbies'. At first, I'll admit, I mentally switched off. We were supposed to be flirting – and he was talking about *hobbies*? But then he told me more about his main hobby: a style of dance from the Dominican Republican called bachata. His passion was unexpected (especially as he was otherwise quiet and reserved) and, as he spoke and showed me videos of his dancing on his phone, I became increasingly attracted to him. He'd actually convinced his employer at a large consultancy firm to relocate him to Madrid – where bachata is popular – and would be leaving the country in the next two months – which is how I found myself boarding a plane to Madrid later that summer. It wasn't bachata, specifically, that interested me (on the subject of playing to your individual strengths, dance has never exactly been my forte) as much as the fact that this man had a colourful life beyond work and seeing friends, which was really attractive. This hobby that he invested time and energy in made him a more compelling person as a result.

Strengthening your connections with others

My friend Siobhan had a bad experience with her ex, but generally the right people in your life will be supportive of your passions, in the same way you must be of theirs. When you ask someone about the things they love, you are both encouraging and respecting their alonement. You watch their faces light up, because you're taking an interest in their soul and celebrating their innermost being. You are at once acknowledging your separateness – your respective aloneness – and your connection. Plus, on a practical level? It makes buying thoughtful birthday presents a hell of a lot easier when someone actually has a hobby.

Having outside interests can help to take the pressure off our romantic relationships, too. Storr echoes Siobhan's wise approach – that you shouldn't rely solely on a partner to sustain your sense of identity and meaning. 'Everyone needs interests as well as interpersonal relationships; and interests, as well as relationships, play an important part in defining individual identity and in giving meaning to a person's life,' he writes in *Solitude*. If we can learn to value this separateness – and to respect it as a value for our partners, too – it can act as a force for positive connection; showing love through encouraging one another's hobbies, for instance, or allowing absence (while you're pursuing your respective passions, apart) to make the heart grow fonder.

Celebrating your individuality

As Storr says, actively committing time and energy to an activity is something that truly makes you stand out as an individual. That's no small feat in a noisy world where we are bombarded with so much information about other people's lives, and what they are doing, that we end up watching them – quite literally, *followers* – focusing on their lives instead of our own. Remember 'rubbernecking', the phenomenon I described in the introduction? Rubbernecking can be when you fall into the trap of spending your train journey looking at someone's holiday photos on Instagram, rather than learning Italian via DuoLingo. It's easy to spend a lot of precious time rubbernecking since, due to social media, 'we've got constant little abstract pieces of information about thousands of people that we met once or barely know,' as Daisy Buchanan phrased it on the podcast, and this information overwhelms us and distracts us from leading our own lives. Those able to avoid this temptation – and to focus on their own growth and personal achievements instead – stand out from the crowd, achieving an elusive authenticity and individuality of their own. Think about it; the most influential people on social media – Cristiano Ronaldo; Billie Eilish; Insta-poet Rupi Kaur; mysterious graffiti artist Banksy – are admired because of the time they spend offline, honing their craft. That's also something I learnt through interviewing an inspirational line-up of authors, thinkers and media personalities on my Alonement podcast; without fail, all of my high-flying guests achieved success thanks to the alone time they devoted to their passions.

It's also through facing forward and pursuing your passion that you discover your unique worth as an individual, and that can be immensely powerful. Take the example of award-winning author Derek Owusu, who explained on my podcast that he spent years trying to emulate other people, from celebrities to twentieth-century philosopher Bertrand Russell. It's only when he started working on his debut novel,

That Reminds Me (after his best friend, writer Yomi Adegoke, spotted his writing talent from his WhatsApps) that he committed to writing in his own voice and 'believing that that's good enough – because it is good enough'.

All too often, our individual interests can fall to the wayside. But prioritising them – simply facing forward and doing your thing – makes you rare and compelling. It could be a weekly pottery class, or pole dancing or powerlifting. It might be learning to play the saxophone, or brewing kombucha. You may not spend the bulk of your hours doing that thing, nor even feel the need to mention it at a party (because ultimately this is more about impressing yourself), but building time into your life to simply 'do you' is a rewarding, invaluable use of your alonement.

6

ALONE AND PROUD

Remember Coffeeshop Psychopath from Chapter 2? I have a confession. I am also that psychopath; you will often spot me conspicuously alone in a public space. I go about life with the general philosophy that I can occupy the outside world as a party of one, with no qualms about celebrating a career milestone with a lavish solo restaurant lunch, or wandering, at my own pace, around the latest Tate Modern exhibition. Don't get me wrong, I love seeing my friends and family, but the ability to go out and have these experiences alone too has been transformative. The truth is, many of us are terrified of sitting by ourselves in a restaurant or taking stealth solo trips to the cinema – so, buckle up.

These days, as the founder of a platform about being alone, friends will send me photos of their delicious truffle pasta while dining for one, or their solitary Martini at a cocktail bar, and I can't help but notice these outings rarely make it on to social media. Why? On a larger scale, there's no *Time Out* guide for, well, time out from other people. If you book a solo spot on an Airbnb experience, a little message pops up: 'Activities are better with friends! Click here to invite them.' Businesses regularly offer buy-one-get-one-free deals as incentives, from Odeon's Meerkat Movies to Pizza Express's two-for-one on main courses. Don't forget the tyranny of small plates or mezze platters designed for sharing among a group.

Like many people, I spent most of my life suffering from a mental block when it came to doing things alone in public. It wasn't that I consciously *feared* dining alone or sitting by myself in a theatre audience; it's that I never even considered it a viable option. But then, one Saturday morning after my New Year's resolution, I woke up and – millennial cliché alert – wanted eggs, sourdough and avocado for breakfast, but didn't feel like cooking it myself. It was 8:02am, and I'd learnt the hard way that not everyone wants to eat breakfast with me at that time on a weekend; plus, I'd designated Saturday mornings for alone time. It was then that something clicked. Just because I'd only ever eaten meals out with other people in the past didn't mean I *had* to now. I realised that, beyond the marketing messages I'd internalised, there was no reason why I couldn't go out to places by myself.

Going to the cinema or dining out alone doesn't mean you never want company again. You don't automatically become

Miss Havisham by booking a table for one. It does, however, open up a whole other way to enjoy things you've done your entire life: you can get into films or theatrical shows without worrying about your companion's response, and you can mindfully enjoy your bun cha without the complication of making conversation between mouthfuls of noodles. Besides, are all public activities conducive to socialising, anyway? 'It never occurred to me that sitting silently in a darkened room was supposed to be a social thing, to be honest,' remarked one of my Twitter followers when I asked about the attraction of solo cinema trips.

If you don't learn to venture out alone, you'll always be reliant on another person to facilitate your pleasure. This might mean you'll miss out on activities you really want to do, or end up dragging a friend to something that, actually, they couldn't be less interested in. Once you have the option of going out without company, you start to focus more on what might be fun for the both of you to do together. Far from being selfish, having the capacity to get a kick out of activities alone actually enables you to be more considerate. I'm reminded of a story of my friend's parents who, upon arriving at a multiplex, realised they wanted to see different films, so they parted ways for the next two hours and reunited for dinner, afterwards, both perfectly content.

Through overcoming my fear of being alone in public, the world became my oyster. My solo adventures over the past couple of years have included spontaneous weeknight trips to the Everyman cinema, bagging last-minute front-row theatre tickets, and watching one of my favourite comedians, Hannah Gadsby, at her Douglas show at the Southbank Centre. But, first, I had a lot to unlearn.

The high school canteen effect

Of course, I'm not the only one who had a long-harboured fear of doing things alone. Think about it: would you feel comfortable doing any of the following solo?

- Going to the cinema
- Having lunch in a café
- Attending a dance class
- Having dinner in a restaurant
- Joining in an exercise class
- Going to a gig
- Visiting an art gallery

I'll testify that old me would have baulked at doing most of these activities by myself. Being alone at home was one thing; it might have felt uncomfortable sometimes, but at least it was a safe space where no one else was watching – but the notion of going for dinner alone in spaces designed for couples and groups felt totally alien and a little punishing. It would leave me feeling naked and exposed. Even waiting for a friend at a pub would make me feel incredibly self-conscious. Think about that scene in *Mean Girls*, when Cady has no one to sit with, so she eats her lunch on a tray while sitting in a toilet stall – as if *that's* a better look than eating by yourself in front of your classmates.

Bella DePaulo, a professor of psychology at the University of California, used to give her students a somewhat unusual assignment: to take themselves out for a meal.* Dining out might sound like a walk in the park compared with an undergraduate dissertation, but the solitary nature of the task – which formed part of DePaulo's 'Singles in Society' course – proved the hard part, with one student describing how her peers were 'horrified' by the exercise. Over the years DePaulo taught the course, more daring students upped the stakes: choosing an upmarket restaurant, insisting on the meal being dinner rather than lunch, or going without a book or anything else to look at.

What DePaulo and her students had identified was that, while most of us feel comfortable being in public spaces with other people, when it comes to occupying them alone it gets more fraught. The added 'challenges' students chose to up the ante shed light on the complex, unspoken rules that inhibit so many of us when it comes to being alone in public

---

* Bella DePaulo, 'The Psychology of Being Alone in Public (Part 1): How Do You Think You Would Feel?' Single at Heart blog, 23 June 2017, *PsychCentral*. https://blogs.psychcentral.com/single-at-heart/2017/05/the-psychology-of-being-alone-in-public-part-1-how-do-you-think-you-would-feel

spaces – systems that totally disappear when you add another person into the equation. The takeaway? In the absence of a companion, we instinctively deny ourselves the joy we can derive from a whole host of enjoyable activities – and, often, we don't really understand why.

Unpacking our fear of being alone in public

You can probably think of a couple of scenarios when being alone in public is a breeze, even if that's just going to the supermarket or to the gym, but there are likely many others where you'd avoid ever being alone. What is it that prevents us from going for a pizza or to a HAIM concert by ourselves, when there's no rational reason? And what is it in our minds that turns an acceptable group outing into an excruciatingly awkward solo one?

In 2015, American marketing professors Rebecca Ratner and Rebecca Hamilton tackled this very question in a research paper entitled 'Inhibited from Bowling Alone',* which consisted of five studies all focused on 'unaccompanied public activities'. They wanted to discover what makes us avoid doing certain activities in public when we're alone. At the time the research was conducted, US consumers were

---

* Rebecca K. Ratner and Rebecca W. Hamilton, 'Inhibited from Bowling Alone', *Journal of Consumer Research* (2015), 42(2): 266–283. https://academic. oup.com/jcr/article-abstract/42/2/266/1816188?redirectedFrom=fulltext

spending more time alone than ever, thanks to factors such as a rise in single-person households, couples getting married later and the decline of formal organisations and clubs outside of work.

This, they reasoned, probably meant there were more people who 'lack an activity partner' for the things they wanted to do: like having no one to go for sushi with if their partner is working late, or not having anyone to spontaneously grab brunch with on a Sunday morning if they live alone in a remote part of town. Yet, rather than bite the bullet and go alone, consumers would often avoid doing certain activities altogether if there was no one to share them with. So, what made going solo so unpalatable? According to their findings, there are three main factors that influence consumers' attitudes towards spending solo time in public:

1. You believe people will think you're a loner.
2. You think you won't have fun alone.

And, curiously:

3. You're worried you'll look like you're enjoying yourself.

Let's unpack these fears.

The fear of looking like a loner

Let's say you've worked late and you're on the train home. You *could* pick up an M&S Egg Mayonnaise sandwich for the third time this week – but, suddenly, that idea feels a bit stale. Walking past the new French place that just opened, you smell the aroma of ratatouille and think, you know what, I'm going to treat myself. Your experience could go one of two ways. Maybe you really go for it, taking time to savour your coq au vin, building a rapport with the waiter and even staying on for crème brûlée (which ends up on the house after you shamelessly schmoozed said waiter). Or, you could fall victim to self-consciousness and fret about what your decision to dine alone in public might say about you. Did the waiter look at you strangely when you asked for a table for one? Is that couple laughing at you because they think you've been stood up? Suddenly, your whole meal is ruined because of the lingering worry of what your decision to be alone in public might say about you.

Although the 'Inhibited from Bowling Alone' study found that many of us worry about appearing unpopular, the researchers identified a double standard: consumers actually had far fewer inhibitions about going solo when it came to doing 'utilitarian', i.e. practical activities that served a purpose. The self-consciousness crept in when it came to 'hedonic' activities, i.e. those done purely for pleasure. So, why do public acts of hedonism pose more of a problem? This is down to the prevalent (and incorrect) social perception that fun activities – like eating in a restaurant – are always more enjoyable with others (and therefore you wouldn't choose to do them by yourself). So, picking up dry cleaning or wolfing down a Pret sandwich alone probably won't make you feel self-conscious, but eat a three-course meal in a French bistro or attend a singalong performance of *Mamma Mia!* at the West End alone, and you might worry your lack of company appears unintentional – like you've been stood up, perhaps.

The spotlight effect

DePaulo carried out a study* to gauge preconceptions about solo diners. She showed one group a set of images of people dining in a pair and showed the other group the same images Photoshopped to make it look like the subjects were dining solo. Then, she asked the participants to comment on what they thought about the diners. As you might expect, there were some negative comments about the apparently solo customers – 'He is lonely', 'She looks depressed', 'Doesn't have

* Bella DePaulo, 'Dining Alone, Part 2: Here's What People Really Do Think of You', *Psychology Today*, 9 April 2008. https://www.psychologytoday.com/gb/blog/living-single/200804/dining-alone-part-2-here-s-what-people-really-do-think-you

many friends' – but there were also a lot of positive comments, including: 'Enjoying a few good peaceful moments', 'She just wanted to eat by herself', 'He seems to be enjoying his dinner'. As for the accompanied diners? Some participants observed that the man was 'having dinner with his wife for fun' and that the couple looked 'very close' and likely 'enjoyed spending time together'. But there were also some more negative comments: the couple were out 'to have a talk because their relationship needs some mending', suggested one person, while another commented: 'She is upset'. The study found that the proportion of negative to positive comments varied very little between the pictures of people dining alone or as a couple. The upshot? We will often judge other people, and make up a narrative about them, but it's actually a myth that you'll be judged more harshly if you're dining alone.

We also suffer from something called 'the spotlight effect', as coined by psychologist Thomas Gilovich. In a nutshell, this means that alone or otherwise, we tend to overestimate how much other people are looking at us. In a 2000 research study,* Gilovich split a number of students into groups and randomly assigned one person in each group to wear a Barry Manilow T-shirt (he had already established that among that particular group Barry would be an embarrassing person

* Rodolfo Mendoza-Denton, 'The Spotlight Effect', *Psychology Today*, 5 June 2012. https://www.psychologytoday.com/gb/blog/are-we-born-racist/201206/the-spotlight-effect

to have on a T-shirt). When he asked the unlucky T-shirt wearers to predict how many people would notice, they all estimated around 50 per cent. The reality was closer to 25 per cent. Being alone in public can feel like a vulnerable experience for so many reasons, and it might feel like you are wearing a Barry Manilow T-shirt (or a Jedward hoodie, just to update this a little), but it's actually more likely that no one's noticed.

The idea that you won't have fun alone can be a self-fulfilling prophecy, particularly if you spend the whole time caving into your (as evidenced, irrational) self-consciousness. So, it's time to shake off these inhibitions and face the liberating reality that time alone in public can be just as fun and enriching as sharing these experiences with others. There's research to back this up. In the 'Inhibited from Bowling Alone' report, Ratner and Hamilton asked two separate groups to visit an art gallery: one group went as individuals, while the other went in pairs. Although the individuals were less likely to look forward to visiting compared with the pairs, after the visit it was a different story. Lo and behold, both groups reported similar levels of enjoyment.

You're scared that people will see you having a good time alone

This one's a little more complicated. It's the fear, not that you'll look like a loser or as though you're not having a good time by yourself, but that people will see you actually having fun, by yourself, in a social space – like you're publicly masturbating or something. This sense of shame intensifies the more people you think (emphasis on *think*) are watching you, so you're more likely to go out and have a good time, solo, if you don't think you're being observed by many others. In other words, greater 'observability' makes us more reluctant to do public activities alone.

In another study from the 'Inhibited from Bowling Alone' research, participants were asked when they would prefer to see a film at a cinema: at peak time (Saturday night) versus an off-peak time (Sunday night). While most preferred to see the film on the Saturday night – when they might normally visit the cinema – this preference changed once they were told they would visit alone, with almost everyone choosing the Sunday night showing. I'll admit, even I'm not immune to this one, and going to the cinema alone on a Saturday night is a frontier I personally have still yet to cross; I prefer off-peak weeknights when it's less busy. And you know what? That's OK. Sometimes we're still working through our fears around being alone. Nonetheless, once you identify and rationalise what those fears are, it's easier to face them. You might, after learning about the spotlight effect, feel empowered to go for a solo slice of cake at Gail's, even if you still feel instinctively self-conscious when you walk inside. Or maybe you'll be encouraged to visit a photography exhibition alone, based on the evidence that it is possible to enjoy activities all by yourself. Whatever your hang-up, it's time to push past your fears and buy a ticket for one.

Standing out from the crowd

My friend Liam, 31, breaks the mould. As long as I've known him, he's had an instinctive knack for doing whatever he wants alone. From ice skating to going to a gig, if he fancies it, he'll do it – no other person necessary. It's not that Liam is anti-social; in fact, he's the opposite. He has a wide circle of friends whom he often ropes into whatever hare-brained scheme he's come up with, whether that's a late-night screening of *The Room* (widely regarded as one of the best worst films ever made – it's so bad it's good) or a whistlestop tour of north London's finest shakshuka spots. But, if no one's up for it, he's entirely undeterred and almost always follows through with his plans alone. 'Since my late teens, I've always felt confident checking out things I'm passionate about,' he told me. 'Sometimes I'd prefer for someone else to join me – for instance, if I'm going to a gig, it's nice to share in the euphoria with a good friend, but I'll happily go without [company] if no one shares that particular interest. If I'm excited to try something, I won't let the constraints of not having someone I know to join in stop me.'

Liam has a wide circle of friends, and an even broader, boundless curiosity for niche cultural interests, from the Beastie Boys to basketball. And his lack of fear around solo activities means he doesn't miss out on following his passions, such as the time he heard the British astronaut Tim Peake give an exclusive talk in London. 'It's about capturing those fleeting moments,' he said. 'If friends don't want to join, and cost isn't too much of a hindrance for myself, I'll go solo, and most of the time I'm glad I did, as the opportunity may not arise again.' A few years ago, Liam's approach baffled me. I remember being incredulous the time a few of us turned down Liam's impromptu proposal to go trampolining on a Tuesday night, and instead he went alone. Back then, the thought of doing everything he did alone would feel so alien it made my shoulders seize up with awkwardness. But, as I began to challenge my own boundaries around alone time, I thought of Liam not with bafflement but with a newfound respect and admiration.

I recently spoke to Yasmin, 28, who actively cultivated an approach more like Liam's after resolving to learn to do public activities by herself. As the only single person in her group of friends, she found herself regularly getting cancelled on at the last minute: 'This meant plans would be made, and broken, and then the thing I had planned to do or visit, or eat, wouldn't happen,' she says. Tired of relying on 'flaky' friends, she decided to take matters into her own hands: 'I realised it wasn't a requirement for someone to be with me in a cinema, or to get a flat white or to see an exhibition.' Instead, Yasmin resolved to visit a different café, restaurant or coffee shop around London every weekend, usually followed up by another cultural activity. At first, this alone time had been a fallback option Yasmin took to avoid falling victim to her friends' flakiness, but she soon found that, far from a necessary evil, public alone time could – in some respects – emerge as more rewarding than time spent with others. 'Most of the time, it was freeing because you'd worry if the other person was really enjoying doing whatever it was you were doing together or just there.' It also – indirectly – led to Yasmin meeting her significant other, whom she now lives with. 'One weekend, I followed my brunch out by going to an art gallery in Bermondsey, where I struck up a conversation with a handsome stranger. Prior to learning to spend time alone, though an extrovert, I wouldn't ever have had the courage to speak to a stone-cold fox in an art gallery.'

While Liam never felt hindered by being alone in public, Yasmin struggled more along the way. 'At first, it was a little awkward. You're used to being with others all the time in those social spaces,' she said. There were also logistical concerns, like the trend for small 'sharing' plates and being given bad seats at a restaurant, but she soon found the pros outweighed the cons. Both Liam and Yasmin reached the same conclusion: that there was joy (and even spontaneous romance) to be found in occupying 'public' spaces alone. Liam, to this day, regularly seizes the moment in the most spectacular way possible, satisfying his innate curiosity, while Yasmin actively took control of her weekends by resolving to do the things she loved alone, rather than being at the mercy of a last-minute cancellation text.

Conspicuous alonement

As Liam and Yasmin found, doing activities alone can be a good back-up plan if there's no one around to join you. Yet sometimes alonement in public (what I like to call 'conspicuous alonement') is more than just replicating the experience you'd have with a friend or partner. Sometimes those public solo dates might hold an intrinsic value in and of themselves, meaning that you can enjoy an experience precisely because of – rather than in spite of – the lack of company.

One of the things I love about being alone in public is being around other people. I know, I know, that sounds like a total paradox, and it took me a while to appreciate the sense of 'alone togetherness' that formed part of the fun. Take, for example, my Saturday ritual of having breakfast alone at a local café. Reminiscent of an English tearoom, but with Art Deco flooring and decorated with framed posters from classic Italian films, my local is a shabby-chic mishmash of homely loveliness, and a thing apart from the chi-chi line-up of cafés nearby. The café is accommodating to solo visitors like myself, as there are lots of covers and I always arrive before it is full. There's even a sunny spot at the back which is perfect for a solo diner. When I started this ritual, it was to help me learn to do things alone; but I came to an un-expected revelation: the strangers I ate breakfast with formed a crucial part of the experience.

It wasn't until the first lockdown in 2020 that the penny dropped. I continued my regular breakfast routine, setting aside every Saturday morning to order poached eggs on sourdough via delivery and eat it in my flat. Food, check. Reading material, check. Nice environment, check (I lit a candle, whipped out a napkin, the whole works). Yet it wasn't the same. While all the usual elements of my weekend ritual were there, what I missed intensely was the gentle exchange of pleasantries with the waiting staff and the buzz of families, couples and other solo diners around me. What was it about the presence of relative strangers that made my Saturday morning so much more enjoyable?

In 2014, Yale University researchers conducted a study*
to investigate the age-old assumption: that experiences are
better shared with other people. Participants were asked to
taste two different types of chocolate (one sweet and delicious, the other bitter and unpleasant). Some participants
ate the chocolate in the company of another person, while
others ate it alone. Those sharing the experiences reported
more pleasant feelings in response to the sweet chocolate,
which seemed to reinforce the belief that we enjoy positive
experiences more in the company of others. But here's the
interesting part: throughout the study, the 'other person'
figure was actually one of the researchers, who stayed silent
during the experiment. 'When people think of shared experience, what usually comes to mind is being with close
others, such as friends or family, and talking with them,'
said social psychologist and lead researcher Erica Boothby.
'We don't realise the extent to which we are influenced by
people around us whom we don't know and aren't even
communicating with.' So, experiences may be better shared,
but you don't have to know or even interact with the people
you're sharing them with.

The science had spoken; I was on to something. I'd never
considered that my fellow coffee shop customers and the
staff were the make-or-break part of my Saturday mornings,

---

* Association for Psychological Science, 'Sharing makes both good, bad experiences more intense', *Science Daily*, 7 October 2014. https://www.science
daily.com/releases/2014/10/141007103433.htm

but there was something about the communality of the experience that helped me relish it even more. Even when able to recreate every other element of this weekly outing from the comfort of my own home, it was being around others that I missed. Grace, 28, puts it best. A keen traveller, Grace has become accustomed to dining alone around the world and, rather than feeling the absence of companions, she has actively come to enjoy it. 'Travelling solo was how I discovered the joy of spending time in a crowded café, and it's something that I've taken into my daily life. I particularly love how well you capture the feeling of being surrounded by the warm buzz of people while also having mental space and tranquillity.'

And that's just it. Saturday morning – my sacred weekly me-time – is when I like to decompress and not necessarily give anything back, to regain my energy after a week of interviewing and socialising. Yet I still enjoy basking in that 'warm buzz' of others. It's almost like the extrovert and intro-vert sides of my personality are united in perfect harmony. Perhaps this resonates and you have also felt this powerful sense of collective oneness, on a train or during a concert or in a place of worship; that comfortable sensation that you are at once alone but also together with fellow humanity. Or perhaps I come across to you like a total creep who likes lurking in the corner of cafés (guilty). Either way, whether you like the feeling of strangers around you or simply don't want to let a lack of (good) company restrict you from living your best life, learning to be alone in public reaps rewards. So, how do you get started?

Beginner's level: the cinema

If ever a public space was tailor-made for being alone, it's the cinema: a dark auditorium with a blaring soundtrack where talking and looking at your phone is basically forbidden. Deprived of all sensory stimulation outside of what you're watching, it's you and the film, my friend. While we're not all down with going to the cinema by ourselves (yet), there's a substantial minority who love to do so: almost a quarter of consumers (24 per cent) see a film alone three or more times a year, according to a Showcase Cinemas survey.* What's more, over a third of people surveyed (36 per cent) said they preferred going to the cinema alone to going with company.

When I polled my Twitter followers on the public places they'd most comfortably visit solo, going to the cinema scored much more highly than visiting an art gallery, dining alone or even attending an exercise class. I received a flood of impassioned responses from lovers of solitary cinema visits. Nancy, 38, described her trips to the cinema as 'a date with

---

* Kayleigh Dray, 'Scared of going to the cinema alone? Don't be: it's a brilliant form of self-care', *Stylist*, 13 January 2019. https://www.stylist.co.uk/life/cinema-alone-self-care-movies-films-anxiety-mental-health-mindfulness/246032

myself to watch treasure or trash. Whether sitting on a plush Everyman sofa or dashing to half price Mondays, solo cinema trips mean no bartering over what to watch, lights down, sound up: pure bliss.'

'Solo cinema is one of my absolute favourite things to do in the world. I can choose the films I want to watch, I go in the daytime when it's quiet, I can choose my own snacks and I don't have to talk to anyone,' added Kat, 35.

Sam, 41, shared his love of the cinema on a bad day: 'The immersiveness of the environment takes my mind off whatever's bothering me. I always come out the other side feeling better.' When I asked him if he would prefer to go alone or with someone else, he responded: 'Probably on my own, if I'm honest. With people (as lovely as all the people I've seen films with are) there's a pressure to talk about the movie afterwards, whereas I prefer a bit of silent contemplation to process what I've just seen.'

As the 'Inhibited from Bowling Alone' research suggests, we tend not to like the feeling that too many people are observing us in public. That's why, if you're not used to spending time alone, the cinema is a good place to start because you're less likely to feel 'watched' (recently, I attended an early evening Monday showing in the presence of one couple and one other solo cinemagoer. Zero reasons to feel self-conscious and maximum enjoyment – and *yes*, I upgraded myself to a better seat.)

Habits can be difficult to break. No matter how on board with being alone you are in theory, they can be daunting the first time you do them, simply because you lack a social script. Who holds your popcorn while you go to the toilet? Say you want to try out a salsa class. Who will you pair up with when you're dancing? (FYI: for salsa classes, you switch partners throughout, so it's basically irrelevant whether you attend with anyone or not.) Who do you chat to before the session starts? The thing is, all of these concerns fade into insignificance once you experience the joy and empowerment of doing things in public alone. Once you embrace the challenge of going to places alone, you'll start to feel a sense of inherent satisfaction in what you're doing. But not every social situation is made equal when it comes to taking your alonement public.

Pro-level alonement: dining alone

Dining alone can be the ultimate luxury. I interviewed Felicity Cloake about this in an episode of the Alonement podcast, and she said, for her, the idea of dining alone is 'aspirational'. 'I've always thought that being a solo diner, there's a glamour about it, because it implies that you've got the confidence to go and do it and you're happy in your own company.' She's right; solo dining, I like to think, is pretty badass in a world where many lack the courage. Raj, 33, agrees, saying he actively relishes the 'air of mystery you exude just by being on your own'. He eats dinner alone 'on average twice a month' in London, sometimes to 'get a change of scene with a book', other times 'wanting to treat myself if I've been working late'. While in London he's likely to choose somewhere laidback 'with sport playing in the background', but when he's travelling he will choose somewhere fancy. 'I have had a few solo date nights and treated myself to a swanky place, with wine pairing and all.'

While some can take solo dining in their stride, others – even the most confident among us – can struggle. If, for you, the idea comes with an unwelcome side order of angst, you're far from the only one. Pope John XXIII – head of the Catholic Church from October 1958 until his death in 1963 – hated the centuries-old papal custom of dining alone so much that he formally discontinued it. 'I tried it for one week and I was not comfortable,' he said. 'Then I searched through sacred scripture for something saying I had to eat alone. I found nothing, so I gave it up, and it's much better now.'*

When I first started my beloved Saturday morning ritual, I would create barriers in my mind, inventing hypothetical scenarios where people I know might turn up at the café and see me there, shock horror, *all by myself*. After a couple of weeks of doing it, I realised I loved it too much to stop. Doing things alone in public represented a conquering of

---

* Anecdotes & Scripture Notes For All Occasions. https://books.google.com/books?id=gT_i7iEwN7wC

my old inhibitions. If learning to stay in on a Saturday night was my gateway drug to spending time alone, making my alonement public – in spaces I would only previously have occupied in the company of others – was a breakthrough. It was with a mixture of thrill and trepidation that I could walk into a café and say: 'Table for one, please.' In a strange way, it was always quite liberating to feel that I had a right to be there by myself.

When I started writing this book, I realised that there was a frontier I hadn't crossed: going to an upmarket restaurant alone. So, during a trip to Berlin, I decided to go all in. I dressed up in a white linen dress and heeled sandals, put on red lipstick and took myself for a solo date at a starch-napkinned restaurant overlooking Strausberger Platz. I people-watched with a pre-dinner Campari Spritz before enjoying a plateful of linguine alle vongole, mindfully engaged in every aspect of the experience – including but not limited to:

- The children playing in the square in front of me
- The deliciousness of every mouthful of pasta
- The satisfaction of releasing a clam from its shell
- The charming, inconceivably handsome line-up of waiters
- The laughter of the group of middle-aged girlfriends having a better time than anyone else there (except, perhaps, me)

- The citrusy sweetness of the Campari
- The fizz of bubbles against my tongue
- The gentle piano music in the background

I also observed, with – I admit – some schadenfreude, the couples who spent their entire meals looking on their phones in stony silence. I don't mean to sound anti-romance, because that's not it; it's great seeing happy couples and I love being one half of a flirtatious dinner date, too. Yet, it's reassuring to see that the romantic ideal of a couple's dinner date isn't always what it's portrayed to be, while a date with yourself can be a world away from the 'sad lonely diner' cliché.

Finishing with a glass of Montepulciano, a homemade pistachio tiramisu and the book of essays I was reading, I didn't want my evening to end. *What took me so long?* I walked away with a heady rush of joy, not just from the thrill of having overcome something I'd previously feared but also from having discovered yet another way to relish time alone. Once you learn the art of solo dining, it begins a lifelong love affair; a way to indulge yourself that relies on absolutely no one but you. Because honestly, you are worth it, and nothing beats the self-esteem boost that comes from proving that to yourself.

Keep the (solo) customer satisfied

It's worth mentioning that the service at this particular Berlin restaurant was brilliant (shout out to Ristorante a Mano), making me feel so much more comfortable about my first time eating a fancy dinner alone. As anyone who's ever dined out alone will know, this is genuinely the make-or-break factor for whether you'll enjoy the experience.

You'd hope that staff would always be hospitable to solo diners, but in reality, this isn't always the case, and there are certain establishments who take a playground-bullying approach to customers who are on their own. My father, who often travels for work, has had a few bad experiences of this attitude. Once, when he asked for a table for one at an empty restaurant he was told all the tables were reserved. Another time, a waiter saw that he was dining alone and said, pityingly, 'You're so brave.' Owing to these bad experiences, he says that the sense of trepidation has never quite left him.

I also learnt this the hard way. In October 2019, I was asked to leave a café – where I'd previously been a regular – because I was sitting reading an article on my iPad alone. It was half-empty, but the owner refused to let me stay there and eat breakfast by myself. 'People like to see families and customers chatting to each other,' she said. I left the café, and never went back, but the story reached national news and sparked a debate about dining alone in public. After such a humiliating experience, I might have shirked away from public alonement, but, as I mentioned earlier, I had caught the bug and wasn't about to let this hard-won joy go. Besides, if restaurants and cafés aren't catering to solo customers, surely that's *their* problem and not mine. (For the record, the café is still very much in business and thriving, and I'm more than a little proud when I pass by and see individuals peacefully reading in the window. I guess the owner has learnt to be more accommodating these days.)

Another thing we might worry about when dining alone is putting restaurants out, particularly if they aren't necessarily designed for solo dining (i.e. no counter seats, meaning you've no choice but to occupy a table for two). I personally think there are two approaches to this. One is to say, OK, you recognise the stress of running a business, so you'll be mindful as a solo customer, opting for restaurants that do offer counter dining or Wagamama-style cafeteria benches or visiting at off-peak times. However, you need to be wary of a sense of Only Me-ism creeping in here; this is your alonement time and it's too valuable to instinctively compromise on everything.

This is food for thought (sorry, I had to). As solo dining has become more normalised (single-table restaurant reservations jumped 160 per cent between 2014 and 2018, according to OpenTable),* the onus is not just on the customer to be obliging, but also on the restaurants to be a lot more innovative. It's not rocket science. Precedents are set elsewhere in the world: for instance, during a trip to Japan I enjoyed eating at an Osaka branch of Ichiran Ramen, a noodle chain based around the concept of 'low-interaction dining', where you eat in a solo booth and noodles are served from a hatch in front of you. Elsewhere, there's a strong cultural appreciation of food that means you'd never do yourself the disservice and indignity of compromising with a bad meal in private. Felicity Cloake recalls a French waiter chastising her apologetic tone after she requested a table for 'just one person'. 'He was actually quite cross about it. What's nice particularly in France is I never thought that I stood out at all eating on my own. There, it's seen as so important to feed yourself well that I was very rarely the only solo diner. It felt comfortable.'

No matter where you are, remember that even if you're not perfectly catered for as a solo diner, you still have a right to be there. The only thing standing in your way is fear. 'I usually feel a bit nervous until I've actually sat down. The more I've done it, the easier it becomes (especially if you don't make eye contact with anyone and imagine what you think they might be thinking),' suggests Rosie, 34.

---

* Tomé Morrissy-Swan, 'Table for one! Solo dining is on the rise, and it's one of life's most underrated pleasures', *The Telegraph*, 12 March 2019. https://www. telegraph.co.uk/food-and-drink/features/table-one-solo-dining-rise-one-lifes-underrated-pleasures

We may not think of going to a restaurant as a typical 'solo' activity, but it allows you to experience it in its purest form, fully savouring the experience and everything that goes into it: the kindness of the waiting staff, the presentation of the food, the background music. Even if you only do it a couple of times a year, I urge you to try it – if only for the knowledge that you can, that you're not reliant on someone else for your adventures.

It's a total power move to be able to enjoy these experiences by yourself, signalling to yourself (and others) that you are enough, alone, to occupy these exciting spaces. As more people are 'just going ahead and dining or travelling alone', it creates its own 'positive momentum', speculates DePaulo. 'When people do those things alone, others notice and they start feeling freer to do the same themselves.'

How to enjoy your solo dining experience

Given how much of an impact waiting staff make, it's worth doing your research beforehand. Of course, sometimes things are out of your control, but, if you can, try to find a restaurant known for hosting solo diners. A quick Google search will help, or else get a recommendation from a friend who's eaten there alone in the past. I'd also recommend taking some reading material as a prop. It may sound like strange advice, but having something there, even if you barely look at it, will feel like a talisman. That said, I heavily advise against taking your phone out, as this will effectively stop you from absorbing any of the experience. The book, magazine or newspaper is half for show, as you'll likely spend most of your time savouring your food or shamelessly spectating a first date.

Another key tip from Felicity Cloake: if you're solo dining, you will very likely be offered the worst seat – next to the toilet, or in a draught. While you shouldn't take it personally, don't be afraid to ask for another. On that note, never be apologetic. That's the admirable 'don't give a fuck' attitude that Felicity took when she was given a seat by the queue while doing a review at a well-known steak restaurant in London. 'I had to eyeball all these people who looked quite cross that I was taking up a table for two,' she told me. 'And I thought "Yeah, I'm going to enjoy this – I'm definitely having pudding."'

And in that spirit – enjoy it. Remember, too, that if you are in a position to be able to dine alone, it is a luxury, and one you won't necessarily be afforded your whole life. One day, you will look back and think, 'Why did I never have a meal out alone, while I could?' So, do it. Savour the moment and order dessert (with just the one spoon).

7

SOLO TRAVEL

A couple of summers ago, I received a selfie from my friend Rachel. In the photo, she's reclining on a sunlounger on a Spanish rooftop, tanned even for her (she's half-Malaysian and her complexion is the envy of all), face make-up free and glowing, halo-ed by the 30-degree sun behind her. Toasting the camera with a bottle of Peroni, she looks beautiful, carefree and totally badass. For a few weeks, Rachel – fresh from the break-up of a seven-year relationship and a family bereavement – had been thinking of visiting Seville for her first-ever solo holiday. She wanted to read, relax and check out the buildings she'd wanted to see ever since doing her Master's degree in architecture. The photo confirmed that she had spontaneously gone ahead and taken the plunge. And I couldn't have been prouder.

What is solo travel?

Solo travel can be roaming on the other side of the world – daring yourself to spend a month backpacking in Australia, renting a car to take you around and staying in hostels – or it can be closer to home, like a local staycation or a weekend break in Paris. You can even be, as Stephanie Rosenbloom terms it in her solo travel memoir, *Alone Time: Four Cities, Four Seasons and the Pleasures of Solitude*, a 'hometown tourist', treating your local area 'as if it were a foreign city' and 'as if there were only so much time to drink it in'.

Solo travel has enjoyed something of a surge in recent years. In a 2019 survey of 1,000 members of the British general public, 13 per cent said they had embraced solo travel more than ever that year, while almost half (48 per cent) said they had gone on holiday alone in the past.* Meanwhile, companies like Flash Pack and Intrepid Travel offer trips tailored for solo travellers. At the time of writing, it's yet to be seen how Covid-19 will affect the sector, but while the nature of solo travel might change slightly, its value will remain the same. For the purposes of this chapter, where you go on your solo 'travel' isn't the important part. It's the spirit of adventure and sense of alonement you take along for the ride.

---

* 'Solo travel – the stats', *Travel Zoo*, 3 September 2019. https://www.travelzoo.com/uk/blog/solo-travel-the-stats

So, you want to travel alone?

Whether it's a six-day beach holiday or a six-month sabbatical, travel is among our most valued leisure time. OK, it may be prime time to take the photos that will grace your Instagram grid or Bumble profile all year round, but, ultimately, that's far from your only motive when you book off that precious annual leave. The aim of the game is to relax, unwind and – schedule-permitting – maybe to grow a little, too. The question is: do you need travel companions in order to do that? Many of us know the joys of going on holiday with friends and family, but I want to talk about how to be brave enough to go at it alone. It's not about weighing one version of the experience against another, but to recognise and celebrate the unique rewards of solo travelling.

While the decision to travel solo is often made as a last resort, 50 per cent of Intrepid Travel's customers sign up alone, and it's rarely a decision they regret. Senior editorial manager Rebecca Shapiro told me: 'A lot of people end up travelling solo because their loved ones didn't have the same priorities or passions. But most end up discovering more inner strength than they knew they had – and a new lease of life. The theme that resonates most is just how transformative solo travel is. The reality is: if you're willing to put yourself out there, solo travel doesn't disappoint. The lows are lower, but the highs are higher.'

I quizzed my Twitter followers on what they had learnt from solo travel.

'Honestly solo travel is my favourite thing to do ever. It's given me so much confidence and freedom and also a lot of faith in myself that I can handle most situations. I've travelled alone all over Europe and Asia since I was 20 and I encourage everyone to try it at least once!' Georgie, 26

'Doing "big things" alone is actually a lot easier than you might think. It might feel unfamiliar, but it's all totally doable.' Frances, 32

'I realised I'm a planner and travelling alone helped me be in the moment and be spontaneous. I also realised that the stigma around travelling solo was mainly in my head and instead I found out how to revel in my own company.' Lucy, 42

'How much you need your time to do things slowly, especially when you come out of the mad London bubble and have endless days to really unwind (and read).' Alexandra, 27

'Life was a more extreme and vivid experience for me when I was on my own. When travelling I was open to newness and tuned in to what was going on around me.' Edith, 42

Still, for the uninitiated, the idea of solo travel might seem formidable. The solution, as with so much of alonement, is simply to feel the fear and do it anyway. It's OK if you take baby steps. Go for one or two nights to start with, advises Clare, 36, a seasoned solo traveller who has taken a trip by herself every year for the past decade. She advises, particularly if you're a first-timer, to prioritise finding a hotel or a B&B that's fairly central, in an area that you'll feel safe walking around in at night alone (ask for recommendations or check it out on Google Maps Street View). Her other pro tip is to try and find a place that has a bathtub, as for her, having an indulgent pampering night after a day of flying to her destination is key to relaxing on the holiday. While that first night can be more daunting as a solo traveller, beginning in a gentle way will help you navigate the initial challenge of an unfamiliar situation, leaving you refreshed and ready to start your trip. Comfort is key when you start solo travelling, and these practical details can make the difference in creating a positive experience you'll want to repeat.

Safety first

The one thing you do need to think about before you plunge in is safety, particularly if you're a woman. If there's one thing that's prevented many women from travelling it's this: the rare, terrible news headlines that all too often become a cautionary tale for why you shouldn't go at it alone. Another thing that has prevented women from travelling by themselves is that, for centuries, it wasn't allowed. As Rosenbloom points out in her book, it is 'exercising a hard-won right' to do anything independently as a woman, let alone go on holiday. She uses the example of eating out, writing that New Yorkers were debating legislative bills about whether women should be allowed to dine without a male escort well into the early twentieth century. As a woman I personally feel a duty to travel alone, because I am part of one of the first generations of women liberated to do so. As with so much of my personal alonement – living alone, dining alone – I relish solo travel ever more for the simple reason that it's something *I can* do.

I was further inspired by the story of author Winnie Li who, in 2008, at the age of 29, was raped while hiking alone through a national park in Belfast. Ten years later, Winnie wrote an account of her experience for *Stylist*: 'A message to everyone who dares to say women shouldn't travel alone'.* Published in the wake of British tourist Grace Millane's murder, the piece went on to explain why Li continued to travel the world a year and a half after her assault. 'My rapist had already taken so much from me, I refused to let him take that as well . . . It saddens me to think that there may be young women who will not be allowed to travel now, because

---

* Winnie M. Li, 'A message to everyone who dares to say women shouldn't travel alone', *Stylist*, 2019. https://www.stylist.co.uk/life/a-message-to-everyone-who-dares-to-say-women-shouldnt-travel-alone/241921

of what happened to Grace Millane. We are not meant to live our lives in fear, shackled by the spectre of "what might happen". Lots of things can happen, and the majority of them are good.'

There was a similarly defiant response in 2016, after two female Argentinian backpackers were sexually assaulted and killed while travelling in Ecuador. The online conversation centred around blaming the women for travelling alone (even though, of course, they were travelling together). In response, solo female travellers posted photos of themselves around the world with the hashtag #ViajoSolo. The upshot? Be safe. Be responsible. But don't let fear get in the way of your solo travel.

Just a handful of solo travel benefits

In my many conversations with solo travellers as I researched this chapter, I heard a huge number of benefits cited – too many to list in full here, but here are the ones that stood out:

- Doing whatever the hell you want
- Being in the moment
- 'Finding' yourself
- Ticking off your bucket list

Let's take a closer look at some of these.

Doing whatever the hell you want

Rarely is the world more open to you than when you're in holiday mode, with a chunk of time ahead of you and (most likely, if you've chosen to travel there) no shortage of exciting opportunities. As anyone who's navigated the sometimes exhausting politics of a group holiday will know, there is inevitably a base note of compromise, whether that's trawling around Laos for 'vegan options' or agreeing to have sedentary 'pool days' at your hotel in Barcelona when you'd much rather explore the local beaches.

When you're alone, you're guided by your own imagination, and little else. During a weekend in Paris last summer, I managed to squeeze in a literary tour, a visit to a feminist street art showcase, vintage shopping in Montmartre, a two-course lunch at Café de Flore and even a lazy evening reading Elena Ferrante and drinking Merlot at my hotel. Jada Sezer seized the opportunities to indulge in all her favourite things on her solo trip to Tokyo. Driven by her curiosity (and *Blade Runner* obsession), she hopped from the famous robot show in Shinjuku to the Samurai museum, and on to the flagship Nissan showroom. 'I remember seeing this big piece of foam being carved by robots into a car shape, and just squealing, "This is so cool!"'

Travelling alone means you can be completely self-centred. Want to change the plan at the last minute? No problem. It doesn't get more alonement than that.

Being in the moment

As with much of alonement, travelling solo ramps up your capacity to be mindful about what you're doing, seeing or experiencing away from the noise of other people. As I found with my Berlin dining experience, travelling and dining alone means you are so much more mindfully engaged in your immediate surroundings. I loved how Vick Hope put this on my Alonement podcast, when she described travelling to Malaysia for a yoga retreat. 'I remember getting off the plane in Kuala Lumpur and having that feeling when the air hits you, and everything you look at you're seeing for the first time ever because you're in a brand new country, and you feel like a baby who's just been born.' For Vick, the crux was that she was alone: 'It's like a fire that starts burning inside you – a feeling filled with passion and excitement – and it's heightened because you're on your own and you don't have to vocalise that or articulate anything, you can just feel it.'

This isn't to say you can't have those incredible, immersive experiences with someone else; but the difference, when others are involved, is that your experiences are inevitably filtered through their eyes, too. After her first trip to Tokyo,

Jada Sezer returned to Japan to travel with a close friend. 'I loved it – but it was different. You're enjoying it with someone else and their own eyes. It's still interesting, but it doesn't ignite every part of you.' Later, she added: 'Solo travel – nothing really beats it for me.'

'Finding' yourself

We're probably all familiar with the Holstee Manifesto – a millennial wall art staple – which reads: 'Travel often. Getting lost will help you find yourself.' The cliché of 'finding yourself' by travelling is a well-established one, and this is partly to its detriment. You might feel justifiably cynical about the idea of travelling halfway across the world to 'find yourself', sparking as it does a whole series of eye-rolling clichés. You might even be thinking about someone you know who went island-hopping across Thailand, funded by the Bank of Mum & Dad and 'found' little more than a Jack Daniels singlet and one of the more exotic STIs on the well-trodden circuit around Koh Tao, Koh Samui, Phuket and Bangkok. You might even (whisper it) be that person.

Clichés aside, travelling alone *can* undeniably be a brilliant source of self-knowledge, as long as you allow yourself some solitude away from 24/7 hostel socialising or group tours. In some respects, travelling alone and having to rely on yourself simply turns up the volume on many of the benefits of alonement, such as the privileged insights you get into yourself and your character. 'I've learnt a lot about my personality,' says Luke, 28. 'I've proved a lot more capable and better in a crisis than I thought I would be. Sometimes, if I'm in company, I have the tendency to shirk decisions and ask other people for advice.' Being in a crisis isn't a pleasant experience, but Luke feels he has 'grown a lot, especially during the hard times like India, where I had no social group. It was very lonely. I had an argument with someone and just cried, and I didn't know why I was upset, you have to work through things on your own.'

It can also be a time for self-growth. Katie, 29, has experienced a total personality overhaul that she's taken into her everyday life, after arriving in New Zealand and realising her whole carefully planned itinerary would have to change due to a storm sweeping the country. Katie learnt that it was OK to be flexible. 'I was someone who always needed a plan. Now I no longer feel like every hour has to be accounted for, so I'll take the time to explore things around the corner and be more curious.' Shapiro agrees: 'I genuinely believe solo travel catalyses personal development. The combination of spending time alone and having a change of scene lends itself to so many more discoveries, revelations and epiphanies. I always end up with so many iPhone notes of ideas when I travel solo. As well as increased confidence to trust my gut instinct and decision-making capabilities.'

Some solo travellers go away with the aim of processing

something specific, and the baggage you take is emotional (thankfully, Ryanair hasn't yet found a way to charge a premium for this). The empty hours that don't need accounting for while you're on holiday can provide a particularly useful window for substantial 'thinking time'. For instance, Vick Hope's yoga retreat came after a long stint of relentlessly hard work, which led to burnout. After speaking to her mother, she realised her frenetic overworking had been driven by a fear of being alone following a break-up. 'A part of that was me plugging up the time to not think about being alone. I remember lying in my mum's arms, and she said: "Darling, I think it's because you've never been on your own, and you're not letting yourself."' Vick's solo trip, and successive solo trips to Mexico, Morocco and Ibiza, represented a turning point where she learnt that being alone could be a source of 'joy and peace'. That's something she brought home with her, too: 'I just took all these trips so I could feel that [joy and peace in being alone] and then once you feel that you learn how to harness it.'

Similarly, Rachel went to Seville at a time when she knew she needed reflection away from her busy life back home, while Katie credits her New Zealand trip with helping her process a difficult year which had seen two members of her close family have mental breakdowns. 'Having that break and taking long drives by myself, I was able to process the emotions I'd felt over the last year and a half, which had been a lot. I would also go for long walks with no music over the mountains, that's where I feel the most me – totally at peace.'

Ticking off your bucket list

One of the best reasons for travelling alone is simply because it allows you to pursue a dream without waiting for someone else to be 'available'. This is what motivated Katie to take the plunge. 'I've always wanted to go to New Zealand, and I had an opportunity where I had lots of holiday and nothing to look forward to in the coming months. I just remember thinking that if I don't book it, it's never going to happen. I realised that the reason I hadn't gone yet was because I was waiting to meet a boyfriend to go with me, and that was so ridiculous that it made me angry enough to book it.'

Because if not now, when? That's the kind of philosophy that, five years ago, motivated my mother in her mid-50s to book a spontaneous trip to Australia. Although she was meeting her sister and niece out there, she spent five days travelling the Great Ocean Road by herself; and, to be honest, she's never seemed cooler (especially because back then I could never have imagined doing the same). Rosenbloom calls alone time 'an invitation, a chance to do the things you've longed to do'. So, if you have the opportunity to travel alone to the place you've always been curious about, then the choice is yours on whether to accept that invitation – or to keep putting it off.

Top tips for travelling solo

Before you pack your bags, here's some of the best alonement-specific advice I crowd-sourced from seasoned solo travellers:

- Don't forget to pack a cheap mini tripod (for taking photos with a self-timer) and a bottle opener.
- Private hostel rooms are usually reasonably priced, helping you to avoid the dreaded 'single supplement', i.e. the surcharge you pay for travelling alone rather than sharing a room.
- Buy a perfume or scented candle as a holiday souvenir. You might lack a travelling companion to reminisce about the trip with, but smell can be incredibly evocative and will bring back great memories when you get home.
- Ask fellow travellers for recommendations. It's a great way to strike up conversation, and it means you're not overly reliant on TripAdvisor.
- Walking tours are also a fail-safe way to get to

know a city, and to meet fellow travellers if you
fancy company for a bit.

- Always carry a book or a Kindle. You might not
even read it, but it's lightweight to carry around
and good to know you have entertainment on
public transport or at a restaurant.

- Dress up – particularly for the evening – and plan
your outfits ahead of time. You'll feel more self-
confident and able to 'own' eating alone.

- Plan your route from the airport to your
accommodation before you land (resorting to an
overpriced cab last-minute is even worse when
you can't share the cost).

- Keep your phone charged and make sure you have
fully charged power banks. As much as you might
like the idea of digital detoxing by leaving your
phone in your accommodation, it's important
to keep it with you in case you need help or
directions.

8

MAKING SPACE FOR ALONEMENT

'A woman must have money and a room of her own.'
Virginia Woolf

'Your grandad needs his shed.'
My grandma, Jean

The humble shed has long been a respected institution in gardens around the world. Growing up, I remember my grandad disappearing off to his shed at the end of the lawn, which was filled with whittling tools and a putting machine. Gardening equipment lined the walls, while a woodwork bench was set up in the middle. Whenever I imagine my grandad growing up, I envision him there in a cloud of sawdust, working on something or other.

When I started thinking about the practicalities of

alonement – where and when to practise it – I couldn't help thinking about my grandad's shed. I remember it as a space that defined him, and one that commanded respect and privacy. No one ever questioned him when he disappeared off to spend time there, and what went on behind those closed doors was usually a mystery – although occasionally magic emerged, such as the dolls' houses he made for me and my cousins. Even after suffering a stroke a decade ago that severely affected his speech, my grandad has continued to spend hours in his shed – a place that has remained a part of his identity. To this day, the notion that 'Grandad needs his shed' is my grandmother's most salient argument for refusing to downsize their home.

It occurred to me that even the phrase 'going to the shed' served as shorthand for having some alone time. It's a self-justifying phrase that has worked seamlessly for generations of married couples to get space from one another, and the benefits of the shed go far beyond its functional purposes. As any good 'sheddie' will know, the shed has always served an unspoken mental purpose, as well; it's a place of serenity and solitude, away from the shared home. The statistics* make for compelling reading:

* Alex Johnson, 'Garden sheds "worth £5 billion to the British economy"', *Independent*, 31 March 2014. https://www.independent.co.uk/property/garden-sheds-worth-5-billion-to-the-british-economy-9225526.html

- 14 million households in the UK have a shed
- 74 per cent of people claim they feel more relaxed when they are enjoying life in their shed
- 12 per cent of people say they're at their happiest when they spend time in their shed
- One in five people spend time in their garden sheds to avoid their partners

Whereas my grandad's shed was used for old-school carpentry and the like, nowadays it's not uncommon for a shed to be used as a home office or a creative space. One of my favourite musicians, Joe Stilgoe, performed live lunchtime sets daily from his den, which he dubbed 'Stilgoe in the Shed', throughout the first lockdown. But the precise function of the shed matters very little; it doesn't even have to be a shed; after all, the classic model is probably a bit draughty and full of residual dust. But the point is its separateness, and its defined nature as a space away from everyone else, all to yourself, with a locked door. The real purpose has always been to spend time alone – and to spend it well.

Man-cave versus she-shed

The notion of a solo space has been often defined in gendered terms over the years. The humble shed enjoyed something of a rebrand in the late 1990s, with the notion of the man-cave introduced in the cult self-help book *Men Are From Mars, Women Are From Venus*. 'Men go to their caves and women talk,' wrote author John Gray. Oh, John, there you go perpetuating the damaging, centuries-old gendered stereotype that 'real men' need time alone to process their feelings rather than seek help (we'll forgive him – it was the 90s). Still, his writing sparked the popular term 'man-cave', used to describe a physical, male-only space to watch sport or play video games. Advocates of the man-cave take it very, very seriously. No, really. Here's a statement taken from the official Man Cave website: 'We believe that every Man has a basic, primal, instinctual need to have a space to call his own. It's his territory. Furthermore, we believe that space should be used to enjoy his favorite activities, whatever that might be.'*

But what about women? A female-centric notion of 'me-space' – or 'a room of one's own' – was introduced by writer Virginia Woolf in her essay of that same title. Woolf argued that it's essential for a woman to have intellectual freedom and financial means in order to write fiction, which boils down to 'money and a room of one's own'. In contrast to the humble shed, Woolf's imagination of a female space was for much loftier purposes. The phrase has since become shorthand to describe a woman's need for a space to sit and think and create, alone, and has inspired the naming of

* 'Man Cave 101', *The Official Man Cave Site*. https://www.mancavesite.org/mancave-101

everything from a feminist bookshop to an all-female co-working space. There's also the lesser-mentioned 'woman-cave' or 'mum-cave' concept, which journalist Victoria Richards championed in a personal essay for *HuffPost*. 'When I'm in that room, I feel like I can breathe properly,' she wrote, later adding: 'The real challenge? Believing we deserve that space in the first place.' *

A shed of one's own

Here's what I propose: a non-gendered 21st-century re-thinking of me-space. The concept of a room of one's own has been dressed up over the years as a space for a sort of mystical creativity; for the enactment of a feminist ideal; or for the performance of masculinity. It would serve us well to think of these ideas – from the shed to the man-cave to the room of one's own – under the wider umbrella of alonement, because alonement is worth valuing, whatever the hell you choose to do with it behind closed doors.

My grandad's beloved shed is just one example of how alonement can be built into the daily fabric of existence, par-ticularly in a shared space. 'Going to the shed' has functioned as a justification for having some me-time, unobserved,

---

* Victoria Richards, 'Why Every Mother Deserves A "Mum Cave", *HuffPost*, 8 November 2019. https://www.huffingtonpost.co.uk/entry/a-room-of-ones-own-every-mother-deserves-a-mum-cave_uk_5dc3f226e4b0d8eb3c903398

without feeling guilty about it. So why not apply that principle to the space around you? You don't need to be writing *Mrs Dalloway* or even changing a bike tyre to build alonement into the infrastructure of your home. All you need to do is accept three basic truths:

- Alonement is a value in and of itself.
- You are worthy of quality time alone.
- A space to yourself will help you thrive.

Lockdown, and the consequential rise in 'work from home' culture, made separate spaces more necessary than ever. A closed door creates a respected physical boundary; an unspoken 'do not disturb' that you don't get if you're working at the kitchen table. While I was thinking about this chapter, I called my mother – as I often do – to bounce ideas off her. This is how the start of our conversation went: 'Sorry, darling, I've got to go because I've picked the landline up in your dad's study and I'm disturbing his thought process.'

The idea of me-space works well in theory and is a no-brainer if you're rich and famous. That's why the occasional story about an A-lister couple opting for separate-but-adjacent houses – like the ill-fated Helena Bonham Carter and Tim Burton, or Gwyneth Paltrow and Brad Falchuk – spark a level of 'oh, if only' intrigue. Equally, if you're in a long-term relationship, having separate bed-rooms can be a godsend. In 2018, a YouGov survey found one in seven couples would prefer to sleep in separate bedrooms if cost and space weren't an issue*, while Catherine Zeta-Jones once said the key to marriage is separate bathrooms. There you have it.

What comes as more of a challenge is divvying up space in your home that's just for you. The starting point, as with so much of alonement, is to justify the need for space in the first place. If you can identify me-space as a value within your household, whether you live with housemates, children, a partner or even by yourself (I'll get on to this later), then that's half the battle won.

It's true that size and cost considerations mean that some of us will have to fight for our own space more than others, but me-space can be just as much psychological as it is physical. It's about approaching that space with intention – whether it's an armchair in a corner or a Kardashian McMansion – that makes all the difference.

From mansions to 'shoebox' homes: Accommodating alonement

In an ideal world, many of us would opt to have a room or two all to ourselves. Sharon, 55, and her husband Stuart, 70, have

---

* Jessica Morgan, 'One in seven of British couples prefer to sleep in separate beds, study reveals', *Independent*, 23 August 2018. https://www.independent.co.uk/life-style/uk-couples-sleep-separate-beds-partner-yougov-survey-a8504716.html

a fairly enviable situation: together with their 18-year-old daughter, the couple live in a 400-year-old listed building in Lincolnshire which they have renovated to accommodate a more independent style of living. Sharon says: 'Stuart has his own dressing area, bathroom and bedroom. If he wishes to sit up and watch football (which I hate) then he will go off to his space and that works well for us. I love nights on my own in bed.' Sharon has a dressing area and en suite all to herself and sleeps in the master bedroom ('which I consider to be my room'), while she uses the 'swim spa' – a sort of swimming pool/hot tub hybrid – where she often takes a book and has a 'staycation' at home. Basically – if there was an alonement edition of the reality TV show *Selling Sunset*, Sharon and Stuart's place would be listed. Sadly, this isn't a realistic solution for most of us.

Comedian John Robins acknowledged this challenge on the podcast. He says: 'My house is too small for two people, so it's just waiting for various stars to align when you can afford to get a place that's big enough.' He adds, 'I think a lot of couples would probably enjoy and benefit from a house that was big enough to give them their own space and I think that's when, especially during lockdown, things can get quite fractured; when you don't have anywhere to just go and sit and stare at a wall.'

So, where on earth do you get this space for yourself – particularly in a small, shared home – if you're already living with a partner or family, or sharing with housemates? We clearly need to get creative. To this end, I contacted two couples in Hong Kong, where space is notoriously at a premium. First, I spoke to Kelly and Tom, both 28, who rent a 150-square-foot (the UK average size for a one-bedroom home is 495-square-foot)* studio apartment in Hong Kong. In their home, which they refer to as the 'shoebox', the pair say they spend a lot of time wearing noise-cancelling headphones and sit back-to-back if they watch different TV shows or films.

I also spoke to Jessie, 31, who shares a 370-square-foot studio flat – a palace, by Hong Kong standards – with her partner, Rhydian, also 31. The pair have been 'smart' about using the space, she says, with a convertible coffee table/dining table and a projector rather than a TV, but in order to facilitate me-space they will often rely on getting outside. 'In Hong Kong, because of the limited space that people have, there's a high degree of use of public space like restaurants and cafés much more so than I've ever seen in London,' says Jessie. The pair also rely on the other having separate interests to give them me-space in the flat: 'Rhydian has band practice on Wednesdays on the other side of town, which I look forward to because I can come home, call my mum in England, put on a face mask and watch a girly movie,' says Jessie. This solution was a

---

* Tom de Castella, 'A life lived in tiny flats', *BBC News Magazine*, 19 April 2013. https://www.bbc.co.uk/news/magazine-22152622

particularly common one among the couples I spoke to. While asking your partner to leave your home could ruffle a few feathers, it's something that can be worked into a schedule if you're both committed to it.

Finding novel solutions

Marking out potential me-space territory when you're sharing a smaller space might involve taking unexpected spaces in your home and making them 'yours'. Harry Potter had his cupboard under the stairs – so roll with the inspiration. Maybe it's an attic space, a bay window area, a box room, a landing, a designated chair or even a beanbag. Whatever it is, having your own space can prove transformative.

Kara, 28, struggled to get her own space in her house, which she shares with three others, particularly when it came to working from home during the coronavirus lockdown period. 'We're lucky that my housemates' rooms are big enough to work in, but mine is too small.' By mutual agreement with her housemates, Kara now has the bay window area of the living room, which she's transformed into an Instagrammable haven complete with a millennial pink chair, a large cheese-plant and a standing desk (fashioned from an ironing board).

Stephanie, 33, an artist and therapist, tells me that, at first, she was worried about moving from her shared flat with housemates into her boyfriend's flat: 'Having my own space is important to me, I crave it, and I've always been very independent so to be sharing a space together made me feel quite panicked and claustrophobic. In my previous flat, I had my own bedroom, which was huge. It had my piano and a desk and enough room to do yoga so I would literally just shut myself away and I wouldn't need to think of anyone else.' However, after she communicated her worries, her boyfriend (who sounds like a good egg) helped her to set up a desk in a roomy corner of the living room, which has since become her space. 'I have my art desk facing a sky window and my piano is situated close to it. I use headphones for all of it so I can be in my own little world'. Having that all-important me-space has allowed Stephanie to overcome her initial reservations about moving in with her partner. 'Now that my piano is here, all my canvases and all my art materials, I literally have evenings or an entire day where I put my headphones on and block everything out whilst he watches films or gets on with his things.'

Sometimes, me-space might not even be a permanent fixture, but constructing it means making symbolic space for yourself during the day. Teacher and novelist Neil, 46, has a 'nook' that forms an important part of his routine. He sends me a picture of his space in the living room which features a comfy-looking mustard yellow armchair, a foldout desk and a large Manx cat sitting territorially guarding the spot. While the armchair is very much a shared space throughout the day in the couple's one-bed flat, Neil says it is 'exclusively mine for that time slot' between 6 and 8am. Having that space and time slot – and a partner who respects it – allows Neil to hit a daily word count of 1,000 words before starting his 'day job'.

In some cases, there's absolutely no way of getting separate space. This is particularly true if you live in a city with astronomically high property values and rental rates. If space comes at a premium, it's tempting to buy a smaller space and make do. That's when it's time to get smart about it. Visual aids can be a really useful way of showing that you want to be left alone, creating an illusion of a locked door where there isn't one. One of the tips from *Indistractable* author Nir Eyal – which he recommends for open-plan office workers – is to put a sign on your desktop that reads: 'I need to focus right now, but please come back later.' Julie Li, Eyal's wife and co-author, wears a light-up 'concentration crown' – purchased for a few pounds on Amazon – when doing focused work at home so that her husband and daughter think twice about disturbing her. Signs and signals like these can create the space for you to focus without the need for confrontation.

Your spare room is your kingdom

If you've got the option, a spare bedroom can be a saviour
to give you solo space, especially if you already share a bedroom with your partner. Victoria Richards is the mother of
two young children and says her me-space – formerly just a
spare bedroom – has 'literally transformed [her] home life',
which is otherwise one of 'noise and clamour'. She says: 'In
my woman cave, I write, listen to music, read and generally
bathe in the sheer, giddy awareness that the space is entirely
and utterly mine. When I escape to my room, it feels calm
and the space feels serene and I'm not frantic or harried or
rushed or anxious, I can breathe out. Even the colour of the
walls is immensely calming.' Her children have learnt to
respect this space, too (arguably a valuable lesson for cohabiting in later life). 'They're not allowed to disturb me there!
It's the rule. They can't come in unless they ask, they can't
bring toys in, they have to knock.'

Depending on size, a spare room can become a temple of
alonement when it comes to working, practising an instrument, reading or exercise, complete with a comfy armchair,
a set of DJ decks or a yoga mat. If you're pushed for space,
you might want to do away with the bed altogether. OK, you
may not win host of the year, but when you weigh up the
value of having a room you use every day versus one you
use a handful of times a year (assuming you don't often have

guests), it's a no-brainer. Other solutions if you're looking to accommodate guests include: a small sofa bed, which usually serves as a comfy couch; a blow-up mattress, which can be stored; or, as one of my Twitter followers suggested, a Murphy bed – which folds flat against the wall during the day. Just like that, a bi-functional room that is 90 per cent pure me-space.

Vick Hope spoke about the game-changing impact of transforming her spare room into a designated study space – which has allowed her to create mental boundaries for work and play. She said: 'I'd never used [my spare room] as a study before, but when lockdown began I knew I needed to create those boundaries as well, instead of working in the kitchen, so I built a desk and tidied it all up. When I close this door that's the day done, and the kitchen is for me to feel like I'm at home.'

Living alone – in solitary refinement

For the bulk of this chapter, I've drawn mostly on others' experiences – but, when it comes to living alone, I'll start with my own. Living alone, at some point in your life, can be a privilege. Away from the noise of other people, you begin to establish your own rhythms and routines. You tune in to your own natural body clock and develop esoteric habits, like sitting in a particular armchair to read or establishing a 'tea regime' (a four-step progression, evolving from a Pukka 'Relax' tea in the morning, a Twinings Earl Grey at midday, decaf Earl Grey in the afternoon and concluding with York-shire Tea's Bedtime Brew before bed. Just me?). You learn to self-soothe.

Your whole home is your shed, and it becomes a sincere reflection of you. You don't have to put up with the over-flowing laundry horse your otherwise-wonderful best friend leaves permanently erected in the centre of your shared living room, nor tolerate your housemate's love of German elec-tronic music. Any questionable decorations, mess or noise will come from you – but that comes with a certain respon-sibility, too.

It took me a while to master the art of shed life; living alone wasn't a one-way ticket to alonement for me. For the first year of living alone, my ex-boyfriend had all but moved in, and so the circumstances in which I found myself living alone properly were difficult, to say the least. I didn't want to be alone; I'd spent a year in this space thinking about having someone else in it. You have to start off by valuing being alone and treating yourself like you would a loved one who was sharing your space. Unless you take this value seriously, Only Me-ism becomes your permanent state; you end up leaving your space cluttered, never making the bed and leaving toast crumbs everywhere, making your space a hell rather than a sanctuary.

For my birthday last year, a close friend of mine bought

me the wonderful book *Live Alone and Like It: The Classic Guide for the Single Woman* by former *Vogue* assistant editor Marjorie Hillis. Although written the best part of a century ago, its main message still resonates. Hillis writes of 'solitary refinement' and argues that there is a technique to 'living alone successfully'. While some of her advice is a little of its time (I fear I won't be consuming a breakfast tray in bed while wearing a 'training négligée and frou-frou' anytime soon, not least because I'm not sure what a frou-frou is), the principle is there: that you can, and should, show yourself respect, dignity and care while living alone. The ghost of Marjorie Hillis will not tolerate you standing up at your kitchen countertop eating a bowl of Cheerios or crying into your ready meal.

Hillis also takes a hard line against clutter – something I've since adopted. Not a single other human entered my house during the months of lockdown in 2020, yet I learnt then just how much my mood was improved in the evenings by having clear surfaces and a kitchen table that wasn't weighed down with the day's tapestry of books, laptop charger, notebooks and various devices. I also tried psychological zoning, which means I have a chair that I only use for reading, and I eat and work at opposite ends of my kitchen table (resourceful, I know).

As those who have lived alone will know, it can take some easing into, especially if – like me – you have DIY shortcomings and a somewhat limited cookery repertoire.

Just getting started? I asked fellow live-aloners on Twitter to tell me what advice they wish they'd been given before they started living alone:

'Sometimes you'll have to cry on your own, but it'll make you stronger. I remember the first day I realised I was truly alone after an awful relationship and would have to get used to crying alone. It was actually incredibly freeing. Now I have developed coping mechanisms and actually prefer to be alone with my feelings. Whatta ride.' Rose, 32

'To get out and go for a walk before you start overthinking venturing out alone.' Eli, 27

'If I had my time again, I would cook for myself. Because it was "just me", I got into the habit of grim convenience food because I thought there would be waste. I clearly forgot about batch cooking' Ella, 29

'If you don't kill the bug now, it will be in your bed later.' Tasha, 30

'There is a witching hour, particularly in the early days and weeks of living alone, where you feel like the loneliest person on the planet. It passes.' Kirsten, 30

'There are lots of weird noises, and when you're alone you suddenly start wondering what they are.' Tom, 29

'Practical stuff makes a difference to the settling in phase. For example, if you're short, invest in a step ladder (I can't reach my ceilings even on my kitchen step and I've got two lampshades I really want to put up!).' Frances, 32

'Routines are important. It's very easy to end up eating dinner at 10pm because you couldn't be bothered to get up off the sofa and you're not cooking for/eating with someone else.' Ellen, 38

Once you are eased into living alone (which may well be the first time in your life you're doing this), you learn to reap the benefits and value it for what it is: an invaluable time for you.

Every home needs me-space

Alonement is, first and foremost, a value, but it's also something we need to build into the fabric of our lives; into our schedules and our physical homes.

Identifying me-space may be just as relevant for the person who lives alone but treats their surroundings as a floordrobe meets dumping ground and barely spends any time there (OK, this used to be me) as it is for a couple who have just moved in together, or a family of four. Alonement is a sanctuary away from the needs and demands of others; and if you can create that sanctuary within your home, even in an unused corner or courtesy of some noise-cancelling headphones, then you'll reap the benefits daily.

9

SINGLE *AND ALONE*

On the sixth day, God created Adam – who initially had a pretty sweet deal. Today's modern bachelor might find himself in a 680-square-foot flat-share with people he met on SpareRoom, whereas Adam had the newly created heaven and earth all to himself, not to mention the precious piece of real estate that was the Garden of Eden. But, within hours, God realised there had been a bit of an oversight. 'It is not good that the man should be alone,' he declared, with the air of a pushy Jewish grandmother at Friday night dinner. 'I will make him a helper as his partner.' So, he created Eve.

Single *and alone*: A branding issue

When we think of being single, we often associate it with being *alone*, and not in a good way. Single *and alone*. The words co-exist in an unholy matrimony. *I don't want to be alone*, someone will say during the breakdown of a relationship. Renowned singleton Bridget Jones sings her anguished, pyjama-clad heart out to 'All By Myself' alone in her flat. Yet, actually, the words single *and alone* have little to do with one another.

For a start, the whole 'single and alone' thing overlooks the fact that there are many other significant relationships in your life, ranging from the close ones (family and friends) to the incidental social contacts (colleagues, the people in your weekly gym class, Twitter and Instagram followers) that all play an important role in our sense of social connectivity. When we say 'single *and alone*' we fall into the trap of amatonormativity. This is a term pioneered by professor of philosophy Elizabeth Brake, which means promoting the importance of a central, romantic relationship above all others. Amatonormativity continues to dominate western society; it lurks in terms like 'my other half' or 'my significant other', as if other relationships don't make up part of your identity, or the other people in your life aren't 'significant'. It's inherent in our assumption that someone only 'settles down' once they meet a life partner.

In the Creation story, it has a particularly gory resonance, as Eve is created out of one of Adam's ribs so that they become 'of one flesh'.

The pervasive association between single *and alone* has been a thorn in my side while writing this book. Some people – and I include a high proportion of my older relatives in this – still misinterpret the alonement platform as a lonely hearts club. But maybe that misconception isn't such a bad thing, because one thing's for sure: being single is a bloody brilliant time for alonement.

Being single and alonement

Spending time alone, as a single person, can be one hell of a good thing. Yet, typically when we describe ourselves (or someone else) as single and alone, we don't mean it in a neutral way – alone means *lonely*. 'So lonely,' sang The Police about a hundred times in their break-up anthem of the same title. 'Lonely, I'm Mr Lonely, I have nobody for my own,' sang Akon in the early noughties (I'm sorry to have put that in your head). So, who's right?

Sure, as a single person there are some key times where you will feel like the loneliest person on earth. I don't want to deny these feelings, as they are valid and true, and there are few things that can make you feel more acutely alone than the aftermath of a break-up. But what might be even lonelier is when you're at the back-end of a crumbling relationship – especially if you're trying to avoid admitting it to others – and you have no one to turn to but your partner. Being 'in bed with someone who you love on many levels but you are realising isn't your person forever' is the loneliest experience of all, shared author Sophia Money-Coutts on my Alonement podcast. 'That is the worst feeling in the world. Sometimes I joke I'd be happy to be single forever, just to avoid that feeling.'

Loneliness can be the feeling of a lack of companionship or when your emotional needs aren't being met by your partner. 'The loneliest I've ever felt was during a relationship in my early twenties, when my boyfriend would constantly cancel on our plans,' shares Liana, 28. Interestingly, Felicity Cloake said a similar thing on the podcast, sharing that some of her most lonely periods have been towards the end of a relationship. You might even feel lonely at times when you're in a happy relationship; a friend confided in me that, while she's content in her relationship of three years, she worries constantly about having fallen out of touch with her close friends. Being in a relationship or even in a room full of other people doesn't necessarily immunise you from loneliness.

Most of us will agree that other people play an important role in making us feel socially connected, and single people are just as much – if not more – part of their communities. When sociologist Eric Klinenberg (another guest on my

Alonement podcast) set out to write his book *Going Solo*, he sought to demonstrate how the state of being unmarried and living alone was 'surprisingly sociable'. 'In fact, people who live alone tend to spend more time socialising with friends and neighbors than people who are married,' he told *Smithsonian Magazine* in 2012.*

So, to conflate being single with being alone doesn't really make sense, especially when you remember that pesky truth that we are all, fundamentally, alone. Sure, it might not feel like it when your couple friends finish each other's sentences. But, really? Every man is an island, and it's up to you whether you make that a desolate wasteland or an idyllic, white-sand hotspot. In this chapter, I want to focus on the ways that being single is a brilliant time for alonement. After a break-up, that hole you feel when your ex leaves your life can become a window of opportunity *if you let it*. In the context of alonement, single *and alone* begins to take on a much more positive connotation. It means fewer obligations and more choices surrounding how you spend your time, both with yourself and other people. Life doesn't have to involve checking the joint monthly planner pinned on to your fridge. Spontaneous weekend in Edinburgh? You're on. Being single means:

---

* Joseph Stromberg, 'Eric Klineberg on Going Solo', *Smithsonian Magazine*, February 2012. https://www.smithsonianmag.com/science-nature/eric-klinenberg-on-going-solo-19299815

- You have more time to yourself during your weekends.
- You end up living alone, or with friends, family or flatmates who live independent lives.
- You might cook meals alone.
- You often travel to and from events alone.
- You don't have to spend time with 'couple friends' or potential in-laws.
- You don't have to be a 'plus one' at terrible events.
- You sleep alone at night (well, mostly . . .).
- You only have one person to consider when you go travelling, or move homes or jobs.

The only thing worse than sleeping alone

As someone who always liked sharing a bed (I'm a deep sleeper and tend to subconsciously delegate 'tackling the burglar/bogeyman' to my bedfellow), I slept badly for weeks once my ex was gone. I romanticised the way we'd sleep, two adjacent spoons in the darkness, his hairy arm around my shoulders. This memory would come to me late at night, as I lay wishing for the warm body of someone I loved to help soothe the whirring thoughts in my brain. But my rational, daytime mind knew the truth: that that calmness wasn't the full story of our relationship. I'd recall all the things I had compromised on out of love, such as the noise of the television he left on at night, its jarring brightness flashing in my face. There were the long, tearful arguments we would have at least once a week, sparring with each other into the night, sitting bolt upright in bed, putting off that serene sleep of my memories because we were picking at unresolved issues like they were scabs. Sleeping next to someone you love, sharing secrets in the darkness or reading beside each other in contented companionship is all well and good – heavenly, in fact – but there is nothing more miserable – more *lonely* – than that terrible night where you pretend to be asleep because you can't bear the fact of them beside you.

I'm not going to play it down, in the early stages of a break-up, the bed will feel too big and you'll miss waking up with them in the morning. It might be helpful at this stage to keep a pad of paper next to your bed and jot down those less rose-tinted memories that come to you about your absent ex-partner (like 'ate crisps in bed' and 'snored incessantly'); give it a few weeks, and you'll come to realise that sleeping alone has its perks. It's easy to forget, while in a relationship, that this time is precious for your mental health, creativity and sleep, and often having someone else there can disrupt your looking after all of that. The time before you go to bed opens up a world of alonement possibilities and reclaiming it can be powerful. As time goes on, it might be an opportunity to establish a bedtime self-care routine. Now, I sleep soundly by myself. I have a bedside table stacked with books and a 'no screens' rule. The time before I sleep has become precious alonement time, whether it's spent double-cleansing my face, speed-reading a bestselling Holly Bourne novel or writing in my diary. I relish these years that I will sleep on my own, in a state of selfish bliss. While I one day might have someone else in my life to merge routines with (although I'll never again agree to TV throughout the night), I feel little urgency knowing that I already sleep with someone I love: myself.

Learning to sleep alone – and liking it – applies to much of relishing your alonement as a single person. It may not feel immediately comfortable, particularly in the wake of a break-up, but it becomes valuable as a space for you, once you reframe it as such. At this stage of the book, I hardly have to stress that alonement, at its best, is a white space where you can figure out who you are, what makes you happy, what keeps you in your best physical and emotional state and where you want your life to go. Despite all of this, the idea of being happily single might remain a hard sell – particularly if you're newly flying solo.

Breaking up is hard to do

For an industry claiming to cater to every 'occasion', there's a serious gap in the greetings card market when it comes to celebrating being single after a serious relationship. Never mind that you've made one of the bravest, hardest life decisions you'll ever have to make, try as you might, you will struggle to find a Clintons card that reads 'Congratulations – you're newly unattached, and you get to spend more time by yourself!' (Although it's worth mentioning that Scribbler now makes a couple of divorce cards; my favourite reads: 'Congratulations on finally dumping that loser!')

Thankfully, I have my friend Zoe, who greeted me with optimism – and a large gin & tonic – the day I broke up with my ex-boyfriend in November 2018. Zoe isn't a veteran of prolonged singledom, having spent a sum total of 18 months of her adult life outside of a relationship. That said, I've got to hand it to her – she used the time wisely. During her (comparatively) brief spell of being single at the end of university, Zoe did a language course in Paris, went backpacking across South America and took a trip across Europe with yours truly before reuniting with her lovely long-term boyfriend and now-fiancé (hi, Chris!). As a result, she's always had a rare appreciation for both sides of the coin.

What was cool about her reaction was that my singleness wasn't a problem to be solved. While a lot of friends might have well-meaningly talked about rebound sex or 'finding you someone', Zoe encouraged me to treat my newfound aloneness as intrinsically valuable. For a couple of hours, I shared in Zoe's optimism, but her wise words went down like a lead balloon as I replayed them in my head while sitting on the number 76 bus home that drizzly November evening, the alcohol buzz of the afternoon fading away. Taking joy in my singledom felt like a foreign concept, and I spent the next week going out every night or sofa-hopping at friends' flats to avoid being alone with my thoughts.

Nothing about being single felt particularly triumphant during the following weeks, as I slept needlessly curled up on one side of the king-size bed and deleted six months' worth of joint social arrangements from my Google Calendar before adjusting my sharing settings. I didn't have a party for one when I had to cancel the annual leave I'd booked for the festive trip to Amsterdam my ex and I wouldn't be taking together, nor did I jump for joy when I had to explain my ex's absence to my grandma on Christmas Day. A painful break-up, particularly if you don't see it coming, can feel profoundly disempowering, painful and beyond your control.

This has a huge impact on how we feel about the time we spend alone, because when it comes to valuing alone time, a lack of choice is a Big Fat Problem, according to Dr Virginia Thomas (who we met in Chapter 2). I caught up with her while writing this book to reflect on her 2019 study,* where she surveyed a group of teenagers about their motivations for spending time alone. Thomas explained that 'in order to be beneficial, solitude must be chosen freely – in other words, not withdrawing as a reaction to social anxiety or feeling rejected by peers'. In short, situations where you are alone but you feel you have no control over that can

---

* University of California – Santa Cruz, 'Teens who seek solitude may know what's best for them', *Science Daily*, 22 March 2019. https://www.sciencedaily.com/releases/2019/03/190322163339.htm

feel awful. That's why staying in on a Friday night when most of your friends are having dinner with their 'other halves' might be a hard period of time to relish, especially if you've recently been dumped. So, how do you rewrite that narrative?

Rebound alert

Neil Sedaka put it right; breaking up is hard to do. The ending of a serious romantic relationship is up there with the hardest, most formative of experiences, a sense of loss which leaves you feeling incomplete and intensely lonely. The cold side of the bed, the memorised phone number you're not allowed to call, the constant reminders of your ex lurking in your life, the break-up admin required to dismantle a shared life together.

Break-ups are tough regardless of who does the messy business of 'breaking up'. As Matthew Stadlen said on the podcast, 'If you choose not to be in a relationship with someone anymore that can still be painful because there might be a lot of things about that person or about the experience of being with that person that you miss. You're committing yourself not to have the company and the comfort of someone else.' Ultimately, I made the decision to end my relationship, but only after months of trying to fight for it. So, when Zoe encouraged me to 'embrace being alone', it felt impossible.

She was right, of course (she's a management consultant; they pay her to be right), but did I listen to her? Of course I bloody didn't – at least, not at first.

You might – like I did – find yourself starring in a series of tragic tableaus, such as but not limited to:

- Woman Drinking By Herself On A Monday Evening
- Wedding Guest With No One To Slow Dance With
- Vertically Challenged Single Occupant Struggling To Shut Her Own Blinds
- Person With Small Arm-Span Attempting to Change Sheets on Double Bed

Thankfully, society has heralded a solution to the pain and suffering: the noble rebound. The term was first coined by Mary Russell Mitford in the 1830s, who wrote: 'Nothing so easy as catching a heart on the rebound.' Typically, a rebound relationship is entered into shortly after another ends, as a means of distraction from the pain and emotional turmoil of a break-up. When we exit a relationship, many of us will try to quickly find someone else to insulate us against the pain of loss. Sometimes it's a fling; sometimes it turns into a full-blown relationship. That's where the term 'serial monogamist' comes from – a person who is in back-to-back monogamous relationships, sometimes overlapping them to prevent them from experiencing the feeling of loss (kind of like six-wives-in-a-decade Henry VIII, but *monogamous*).

Seeking out a new partner straight after a break-up can be actively encouraged by our friends, particularly if they themselves are coupled up. Real-life break-up responses, crowd-sourced on Twitter, include:

- 'Go back to him – otherwise you'll end up alone.'
- 'Maybe you could just be a cat lady.'
- 'It's OK, you'll find someone else.'
- 'You'll probably get back together.'
- 'You could get someone better than him.'
- 'You should try online dating.'

Angelica, 29, who broke up with her boyfriend of five years at a time when all her close friends were in relationships, told me: 'I don't think any of my friends said this is a great opportunity to work on yourself. They were like, "It will be fine; you'll meet someone else." I was telling them that I'm feeling a huge void, and their solution was to fill the void – by finding a new boyfriend.'

This struck a chord. When my relationship ended I remember feeling the same void, manifested by the cold side of the bed where my ex had once lay as we shared every fleeting thought or planned out days, weeks, a lifetime together. In the wake of our break-up, the sense of loss gnawed at me like a dull ache. Back then, being alone (and having to contemplate this feeling) was my biggest fear. I decided the only way I could avoid this loneliness was to get into another relationship – fast.

Shortly after my break-up, I'd find myself scrolling Hinge on Friday nights, negotiating the moral grey area of using a profile photo taken by my ex. Maybe on some level I knew, as Angelica admitted to me, that 'downloading dating apps is a plaster rather than a solution'. But, honestly? I wasn't sure how to navigate the alternative.

The bad date that changed everything

Three weeks after my serious break-up, I went on a restaurant date with a jeweller. Things were going well – we shared a dry sense of humour and a taste for the same music – until he announced he had to dip out early to go and meet his friends in Soho, casually suggesting I wait for him at his flat nearby until he got back. And they say romance is dead.

If I'm honest, I'd put up with worse in the past; but, this time, something snapped. Maybe it was because I'd just got out of a respectful, long-term relationship, so I could no longer put up with this level of slimeball. Maybe it was because I finally realised that there were much worse situations than returning to (my own) bed single and alone that evening. I just couldn't bend myself like a Slinky toy to accommodate this man, unremarkable in all but his audacity.

What upset me was not so much his behaviour, but more the notion that putting up with it was, potentially, the price I'd have to pay for my fear of being alone. If that was the kind of panic-partnering that loneliness might lead to, then Houston, we have a problem. It was time to raise my standards and to face my fears.

Towards the end of my relationship with my ex-boyfriend, I'd begun to have a similar revelation. We were suffocatingly co-dependent and, as it gradually became clear that we weren't compatible, I clung on to him for the reassurance I'd learnt to rely on him for. This wasn't healthy. I was beginning to realise that my fear of being alone wasn't just a sign of my sociable, loving nature; it was something that could compromise my happiness, compelling me to stay in the wrong relationship because I was so scared of the alternative. At a time when friends were moving in with long-term partners, I felt like I'd fallen behind. But something had shifted. I could no longer let my long-term happiness be collateral to my fear of being single. I was no longer prepared to settle for less just because I felt like I'd slipped down some illusory Snakes and Ladders game where the end point was monogamous cohabitation.

One month later, towards the end of January 2019, I wrote a post on my personal blog, announcing a belated New Year's resolution to learn to spend time alone and like it. This wasn't, as some misinterpreted it, a vow of celibacy or even a dating hiatus. It was actually nothing to do with my love life, although it *had* been prompted by that bad date. 'Choosing to spend time alone has always felt like a self-imposed punishment where you are put in a pressure cooker with your own thoughts,' I wrote. 'And yet, my New Year's resolution is to learn to be alone and enjoy it.' The post's title? Alonement.

The danger of our relationship obsession

Think about what I said about greetings cards earlier in this chapter. You'd be hard-pressed to find a card that read: 'You got divorced!', 'Congratulations on your break-up' or 'Home sweet home (alone)!' Overwhelmingly, the life decisions that garner the most social approval are romantic ones; and this is where it becomes insane. Let's say I'd forgiven the awful jeweller, or, God help me, agreed to wait in his flat like a glorified prostitute (although not even – I'd insisted we went Dutch), told him 'I want you, I need you, oh baby, oh baby' (and if you read that in the deadpan tone of Kat Stratford from *10 Things I Hate About You*, we'd most definitely get on). Say he became so enamoured with the rare and wonderful way I tolerated his BS that he declared, 'This must be love,' and proposed. This, my friends, would be the most socially applauded thing I could do in the eyes of many – so much more than walking out of that god-awful date, telling him where to go, or even getting this book deal.

I'm not the first to make this observation. Author Catherine Gray remarks in *The Unexpected Joy of Being Single* that 'an unattached person buying their home single-handedly will not get the same plaudits, the same social attention, as one getting engaged'. Sophia Money-Coutts, an Alonement podcast guest, observes in her book *The Wish List* that there's no greetings card that reads 'She said NO!' Within this context, relationship breakdowns feel like a failure: a failure to conform to a socially acceptable standard of achievement. 'My strongest emotion when my five-year-long relationship broke down was embarrassment. I think it was an age thing; being single is something you're meant to have grown out of,' shares Angelica.

Romantic relationships are put on a pedestal that sustains an entire industry, from greetings cards to weddings; and, of course, the perpetuation of the human race. It's not hard to understand why this is seen as worthy of celebration. Plus, everyone enjoys a good love story. But if you ever want to debunk the 'relationships are better' myth, speak to your friends beyond the honeymoon stages of their relationships. 'Yes, I'm happy – but I keep fantasising about having a weekend at home by myself, drinking rosé on my sofa in my bachelorette flat with a box set,' says Sophie, 33, now married, in between soothing her one-month-old son to sleep.

It's true that weddings are fun, babies are cute and the sight of an old couple holding hands as they walk down the street is likely to melt even the most hardened of hearts. But it's pretty dark that we value romantic relationships above all others – including – and especially – the relationship we have with ourselves. Society tells us it's not *enough* to have close relationships with your family, or a brilliant group of friends. It's not *enough* to love yourself. This is amatonormativity – the term I used earlier to describe society's fixation with romantic relationships – at play. As a result, there's a temptation to perpetuate broken or unhealthy relationships at the expense of your own happiness and life satisfaction.

This doesn't solely influence singles second-guessing their decision to walk out on a date; it also affects couples. Amatonormativity can be enforced in an everyday way, undermining couples' need for independence, individuality and separate relationships outside of their coupledom: *Where's your girlfriend? When can we double date? Oh, you don't live together yet?* It also might manifest itself in a more sinister way, making those in an unhappy relationship put off ending it out of a fear of being single. Amatonormativity is like the abusive partner that whispers in your ear: 'You'll be nothing without me.' And this only serves to intensify the fear of being single *and alone*.

The worst reason to stay in a relationship

I once read that lying is controlling someone else's version of reality. Staying with someone out of a fear of being single – and facing up to whatever that might mean to you – is doing more or less the same thing. There are a thousand great reasons to be in a relationship. Shared values. Mutual kindness. Wanting to start a family. Mind-blowing sex. A Two Together railcard. A fear of being single *and alone*, however, is not one of them. To assess whether this is what's going on, it's important to:

1. Be on speaking terms with your own mind (whether that's through journalling, confiding in someone you trust, etc.)
2. Actively address any fears around being alone

Without doing this, a fear of being alone will inevitably control your romantic life, likely speaking more loudly than your innermost needs, desires or gut instinct. As Jada Sezer shared on the podcast, 'decisions shouldn't be driven by fear', so ask yourself – particularly in the early stages of dating – do I *want* to be with this person? Or am I just here to avoid being single and alone? If the answer is the latter, you're doing both of you a disservice.

Discovering the single positivity movement

There's an alternative to amatonormativity, and that's the single positivity movement, which reflects a growing conversation around the experience of being single and how it can be a positive, fulfilling status. Its celebrity advocates include the likes of Lizzo, Ariana Grande and 'self-partnered' pioneer Emma Watson. Grande gave a single-positive speech at the 2019 Billboard Awards, months after the end of her engagement to Pete Davidson. 'I look forward to hopefully learning to give some of the love and forgiveness that I've given away so frivolously to men in the past to myself,' she told the crowds, channelling the energy of her hit single 'thank u, next' ('Plus, I met someone else / . . . this one gon' last / Cause her name is Ari').

One of the main voices driving the single positivity conversation in the UK is Nicola Slawson, the founder of the UK-based newsletter The Single Supplement. When we spoke, Nicola said, 'I don't know if the two [single *and* alone] go hand in hand. I know some single people who go on dates three or four times a week – with that, and a full-time job, plus seeing friends, you're hardly ever alone.' This is especially true if you fear being alone. As a single person in my early twenties, I was initially never alone because I came up with all sorts of creative ways of being around others: back-to-back dates, moving into a noisy flat with four other flatmates, latching on to social occasions if I happened to have a free night at the weekend. And – honestly – it never even occurred to me that I had any other option, because then I would be the worst thing possible: single *and alone*.

On the Alonement podcast, I had the pleasure of interviewing Shani Silver, a Brooklyn-based writer and host of the single-positive podcast, A Single Serving, where she interviews single women from around the world. Shani agrees that 'the words single and alone have both been used societally in a negative format, and almost exclusively,' and similarly to Nicola, Shani is motivated by a need to offer a better narrative to single women that doesn't revolve around the 'solution' formula of dating content: 'We're corralled towards couplehood our entire lives; there are so many messages and stories and so much praise given to people who are in couples and families. I want to alleviate some of that stress and pressure by acknowledging that being single isn't a problem, it's a way of life that's really enjoyable.'

While Shani says she would be more than open to a relationship if someone suitable came along – 'I myself want a relationship and I look forward to that one day' – she refuses to let her life be 'misspent' in the meantime. 'If you're single and you spend all your time trying to find someone, then you're trying to get out of this as fast as possible. I think we should cherish every moment that we have to be just completely comfortable and selfish and do whatever we want, it's delightful and I'm not ashamed of admitting that. I'll be in a relationship one day, but I don't want to wake up in that relationship and think that I misspent my time alone.'

There are obvious parallels between the alonement and single positivity movements, not least because they both take a status that has historically been a source of pity and give it new meaning. Like Nicola and Shani, I too feel being single needs a rebrand, and for me that involves the practical step of reframing the 'alone time' associated with being single not as a gaping void, filled with loneliness, but as a floor-to-ceiling window of bright opportunity.

Choosing to be 'happily single'

The single positivity movement promotes the idea of being 'happily single'. This isn't the same as being permanently single, or even single for a prolonged period of time; it's about learning to find satisfaction and meaning in your single state, rather than treating it as a waiting room for the rest of your life. Shani put it really well when we spoke on my podcast: 'If you are afraid of being on your own, you will take the first relationship that comes because it's better than being single but I don't think that it is; I only think the right relationships are better. Once you've experienced the good of being single, I believe you are so much less likely to enter into a relationship that isn't right for you.'

Practising alonement is a huge part of single positivity,

simply because once you know what it is to spend alone time well, it's easier to choose being single – and the potential for increased alone time – over being in a bad relationship. On the podcast, Florence Given used the metaphor of 'making your own cake', which means satiating your own needs, rather than expecting someone else to do it for you. 'You need to spend time alone, you've got to live your life as if no one is going to come in and save you,' she said. 'You learn that you can make your own cake.' A positive relationship, to extend this metaphor, would simply be the cherry on top.

Frances, 32, shares how she began to rediscover herself in the six months leading up to her break-up, writing blog posts and journalling to work through her feelings. Beforehand, she had been neglecting these self-improving habits, her energies absorbed in 'saving' a four-year relationship with her then-boyfriend, who had suddenly got cold feet around their dreams of buying a house together. She says: 'I'd been putting too much focus into trying to fix my relationship with him and I completely started to neglect my relationship with myself.' Ultimately, through her alonement, Frances found the strength to leave her partner. 'I realised that my ex had completely disregarded my wants and needs. I wanted something better than that and decided I can have better than that on my own. I thought, *I need to create an environment where I don't feel this bad.* Because it had reached a point where I was feeling bad all the time.'

Having saved up all her adult life to become a homeowner, Frances decided to spend her savings on a smaller one-bed flat, instead of the house she'd planned to buy with her ex, a decision she describes as 'very liberating . . . it's so nice to think all this space is mine'.

Once you make being single a literally and figuratively safe space, it's easier to trust your gut instinct when it tells you a romantic situation isn't right. A few months into being single, I came to a strange crossroads. As mentioned earlier in this chapter, when my relationship had ended the previous November I'd imagined I was sliding down a game of Snakes and Ladders – the 'ladders' being all the heteronormative milestones I once thought I would have 'achieved' before reaching 30. In coming across the longest snake on the board, I was right back to square one. I consoled myself that at least now I knew what I wanted from a partner. That I would be on an accelerated course within the dating game, as I was equipped with this set of criteria. I even had a literal list: tall, dark, handsome (I know . . .), a foodie, a few years older than me, reads for pleasure, goes to the gym and likes things tidy. But when I started my Alonement journey in January 2019, my romantic outlook shifted a little, as I was now looking for a partner to 'stand together' with; someone independent who knew what he wanted from his life, so our journeys could proceed alongside one another. I was still dating and looking; I just needed someone who fitted my criteria.

Woody Allen once said, 'If you want to make God laugh,

tell him about your plans'; and, just like that, the universe played a practical joke on me. A friend introduced me to Doug, a person who exactly – almost uncannily – fitted my description for The One. For six months, I'd been waiting to meet someone like him. He was charming, considerate and wanted me to be his girlfriend. Yet, weeks into meeting him, a brief spell of infatuation was followed by sudden, inexplicable, resistance. In psychology, they call it SRS (Sudden Repulsion Syndrome). On *Love Island*, they call it 'the ick'. An interesting thing had happened: my gut instinct kicked in, giving me the powerful, unshakeable conviction that I couldn't be with him, however perfect he seemed 'on paper' (*Love Island* informs so much of our modern-day love vernacular; it is what it is). It was an entirely new phenomenon for me, as my gut instinct was something I'd never been aware of before my alonement journey. This isn't a coincidence; as I mentioned earlier, solitude-related practices, such as mindfulness and keeping a journal, are linked with strengthening one's gut instinct.* Anyway, suddenly all I wanted was to be back to myself.

The night I ended things with Doug, I struggled to sleep. Part of it was a feeling of irrational guilt, but there was something else, too, that I needed to untangle. I realised that, for the first time in my adult life, I was truly happy to be single. I felt complete, regardless of whether or not I was

---

* Amanda Kohr, 'What's a "Gut Feeling," Really? (And What Is It Telling You?)', *Repeller*, 12 October 2019. https://www.manrepeller.com/2019/12/intuition-gut-feeling.html

in a relationship. In the past, I'd approached dating from a place of fear; reasoning that something not working out would represent failure. Now that I'd overcome that fear, I was finally able to hear what *I* wanted, rather than let that voice be drowned out by my gratitude and relief that someone wanted to be with me. It was a new and slightly daunting feeling, but I knew I wanted to hold on to it. So, I wrote myself a letter:

I'm not miserable – or lonely – like I thought I might be. Nor do I regret my decision. I'm learning to have faith in myself, and I know I've done the right thing.

A little part of me is worried; worried I won't find my person. But I think the greater worry is that I'm realising I am my own person. That another person can't fulfil my life, and I have to do that of my own accord. When faced with the magnitude of that, I kick against it, instinctively. It would be so much easier, it seems, to believe the myth I've been sold all my life – that love and marriage could save me – but I've come too far. It's like I've let a door slam behind me and now I'm locked out.

The scared child in me wants to believe that, one day, someone can wrap their heavy arm around me and offer stillness and solidity for the rest of my life. But I know that's not the case; on some level, I've always known that. I'm afraid of being alone and yet I know it's an essential human condition. I am scared of trusting in my own power.

Another part of me is excited; a restless child fizzing with excitement the night before Christmas, with no clue what might be waiting for them beneath the tree, hidden in queerly shaped bundles dressed in metallic wrapping paper.

I am in control of my life – and I don't have to wait for anyone to save me. There is something so freeing and liberating about that. I don't need to answer to another person. I am free of obligation; I am independent in the world. Maybe I can't sleep because there is so much excitement ahead of me – and all I have to do is remember that my power lies within me, not in someone else.

Making time for alonement as a single person

As I've said before, alonement doesn't just *happen*. You have to proactively make time for it when you're single, otherwise you might waste a golden opportunity for alonement. As a single person – particularly if you're fresh from a break-up – you will have windows of alone time that you wouldn't have in a relationship, and while there may be a temptation (or at least a social pressure) to say yes to any old thing, carving out time for alonement without apology will be invaluable.

There is, of course, a notion to feel that you *should* be out all the time when you're single, putting yourself in the way of Cupid's bow just in case but, as Sophia Money-Coutts said on the podcast: 'There's nothing better than a night in alone with a takeaway – it's my favourite thing to do – but I used to feel a bit sad doing it when I'm single. I'm over that now.'

I don't know who needs to hear this right now, but a night in *can* be a whole lot more fulfilling than accepting a pity invitation to watch your friend's boyfriend's five-a-side football match because 'you might meet someone'. Being single is a time for cooking the food *you* like without catering for a partner. It's a time for sleeping alone peacefully. In Jada Sezer's experience, being single is a really good time to 'be unapologetic and fall in love with yourself' and to carry out what she calls 'self-work'. For Jada Sezer, her two years of being single before meeting her partner Tyson were 'one of the best times for figuring out who I am and what I love'. It also allowed her to discover a love of alone time – 'If I didn't take that time for myself, I wouldn't realise how much I valued it and needed it' – and to 'bring so much more to the table' in her present relationship.

Here's how other people spent their new-found alonement time:

'Reading, writing and cycling are all activities I've come to fall in love with again now I'm single. These small individual activities are things which I do alone, thoroughly enjoy and find give me the time and space to think and feel at peace.' Sam, 27

'I started a weekly Spanish course.' Liana, 28

'I went full on *Eat, Pray, Love* after my biggest break-up. It was amazing. First, I went to a yoga retreat in Malaysia. Then, I got a job teaching English, all over Italy at various summer camps, before going travelling in Thailand with two girls from America.' Nicola, 35

'Watching exactly what I wanted on telly (no negotiation needed) with wine and a large bag of salt and vinegar Kettle Chips. Bliss! Also: home facials; getting up early to study a language; time with friends. Choosing what colour to paint the walls was also easier, almost fun . . . !' Edith, 42

A word on dating

I thought long and hard about including this section, because there's enough dating advice out there for single people and I didn't want to contribute to the deafening cacophony of content aiming to 'help' people overcome single-itis. So – to clarify – this isn't that, and I recognise that at some life stages (and, for some people, their whole lives) dating isn't, and should by no means be, a priority. Yet, I've dated people on and off over the past couple of years since I made that new year's resolution to learn to enjoy time alone, and I want to share how much that personal journey transformed my dating life. For me, valuing alonement doesn't mean taking a hardline stance against dating; it's about dating with a new, empowered perspective and, if my experience is anything to go by, it's a hell of a lot more enjoyable to date that way.

I used to feel a chronic victimhood surrounding my love life. Looking back, it's no wonder. I've been dumped by text. Dumped after a week of ghosting. Dumped at a New Year's Eve party in front of all of my friends. Dumped in Costa Express before breakfast. And I've been cheated on by two boyfriends in succession. This might sound like I have terrible luck, but I can see now it was down to a combination of factors: a) I was almost always dating someone; b) I was a needy, insecure person; c) I was so scared of being alone that I let anything pass. In contrast, dating with alonement in mind has been an almost relentlessly positive experience (post-Jeweller-gate). I'm still on friendly terms with most of the people I've dated, and I feel like there's always been an undertone of mutual respect.

So, what is it about alonement that changed my dating 'luck'? When you come from the baseline of liking yourself and your own company, and hopefully – after reading this chapter – feeling more content with being single, then the dating goalposts immediately shift. As Jada Sezer so wisely said on the podcast, 'Being happy in who you are stops you from acting out of a space of fear and avoidance,' and that's because you're no longer in the vulnerable position of wanting someone, anyone, to save you from your own company. If it doesn't work out, then you're left with someone you love: you.

Having a relationship with yourself radically changes dating. I had a candid conversation last year with someone I was seeing that went: 'We work on paper, but we don't quite . . . work, do we?' We're now good friends, and I think that stems from a mutual understanding that not-quite-fitting with someone romantically has nothing to do with your individual self-worth. If something doesn't work out quite like I want it to, I'm disappointed, but I'm also happy to return to myself, experiencing the same sense of comfort as when you walk in through your front door after a week away from home.

It comes back to that all-important word: choice. What I've learnt from alonement is that I choose to date people who are basically kind and secure people, because those are qualities I value in myself. I also look for people who are at ease in their own company or who I at least think will respect personal boundaries (because, again, these are characteristics I value in myself, and it takes a mutual understanding for that to work in a relationship). My standards are higher, but that's OK; I'm in no rush to get away from me. This mentality makes dating a whole lot more fun, as your focus instinctively shifts from 'Am I good enough for them?' to 'Would this person be a potential romantic partner?' Once in a blue moon, the answer will seem like yes from the word 'go', but often it's more, 'I'm not sure yet, but they're fun to spend time with and I'd like to give things a chance' – and occasionally it's 'HELL, NO'.

When you don't spend the whole time worrying whether this person will 'save' you from loneliness, dating can teach you more about yourself and what you might want from a relationship. I understand that this isn't the case for everyone, and for some it's simply not authentic to put themselves in lots of unfamiliar dating scenarios. But I've always really enjoyed meeting new people, and dating is a chance to do that. In fact, dating can be an ample opportunity for putting forward an updated version of yourself, in the same way as starting a new job or entering a new social setting can encourage self-growth. I spoke to Florence Given about this on the podcast. She said: 'I go on lots of dates (outside of lockdown). I love learning about myself through other people, and I've learnt so much about my emotional triggers and what makes me uncomfortable, and then I go home and I think, "Why did that make me feel uncomfortable?"'

If you do feel you're ready to date, here are my two golden rules:

1. **Only date when you're in a good mindset:** Not when you're hungover, not when you're feeling vulnerable and definitely not past 11pm. You wouldn't go food shopping when you're starving, so don't scroll when

you're thirsty. Go in with the confident, self-assured energy you'd want to receive back.

2. **Take it easy:** The reason for this is that you don't want dating to become your hobby. You want your hobbies to be your hobbies. Even if you're lucky enough to be receiving multiple date offers on apps, I'd suggest a maximum of a couple of first dates a month (and see where it goes from there).

Your 'Happily Ever After' begins right now

It's drummed into us from childhood that Happily Ever After is something that happens when you meet 'the right person'. As we get older, particularly after A Certain Age (and this can vary depending on your culture or community), single is regarded as a maligned state. But, from an alonement perspective, it's the opposite: a valuable opportunity for self-growth, to work out what you love – from small insignificant everyday things to greater passions – as well as showing love to yourself. If there's one point you take away from this chapter, I want it to be just how valuable your single life is.

Romantic relationships can be wonderful, as I'll discuss in the next chapter. The first year of my most recent relationship was, at the time, one of the happiest of my life, but the period since we broke up, when I've been largely single, has been better still. Single life – particularly once you've developed a certain degree of self-confidence and curiosity for life – is a precious space in your life where alonement is, in many ways, more straightforward and certainly easier to practice naturally. I encourage you, if you are single right now, to value it. Because it won't last forever – and I say that not as a consolation, but as a warning. Don't take this time for granted.

10

ALONE, TOGETHER

Jessica matched with Theo on Bumble and, after exchanging a few flirtatious messages, they agreed to meet for a drink, which turned into drinks, which turned into an adult sleepover at Jessica's. When they woke up, they were happy to discover their mutual attraction extended to the morning after. *It was as if they'd known each other forever.* Both in their mid-twenties, Theo was the last one of his friends to get into a serious relationship, while Jessica, a serial monogamist, had recently been dumped out of the blue by her boyfriend of five years. The first two months were idyllic; they practically moved in together after that first evening and were soon posting cute pictures of themselves on Instagram, cooking romantic candle-lit dinners and driving off for a weekend together in Bath.

But problems started to creep in by month three. Jessica – caught up in the throes of the honeymoon phase – forgot to wish one of her best friends happy birthday and they fell out, while Theo's performance in his sales job suffered so much that he was put on probation at work. Things weren't quite the same between them, either. Feeling excluded from her friendship circle, Jessica became more and more dependent on Theo and would send him strings of text messages when he stayed late at work trying to boost his performance. Meanwhile Theo, who would typically travel home via the gym to lift weights, had started to neglect his regime in favour of getting home to have dinner with Jessica and found his self-esteem rapidly deteriorating as a result. Their declining self-confidence seeped into all areas of their lives, and cracks began to show in their relationship. They lashed out at each other, scapegoating the relationship for the parts of their lives that weren't going right. By month six, they had split up – with Jessica feeling estranged from her friends and Theo a stone heavier and barely hanging on to his job.

A lack of alone time isn't simply unwise in a relationship; it can often be the ruin of both the budding romance and the people in it. We're sold the myth that 'love conquers all', but that can mean we pile a whole lot of demands on would-be partners, putting a strain on what would otherwise be a great thing. If there was one commonality among all the happily coupled up guests I had on the podcast, it's that they made time and space for alonement in their relationships. As Alice Liveing said, 'We both live our own lives. I'd never like to live in someone's pocket or to be one of those couples that does everything together; it would be suffocating.'

It's easy to lose perspective during the first days of a relationship and spend inordinate amounts of time together. But, over time, relationships can become habit-driven, like 'comfortable slippers', says psychologist Emma Kenny, and you start to rely on your partner for everything (a model known as co-dependency). Eventually, this means you take no time for yourself outside of the relationship. Why spend the whole evening at the gym, or stay late at Happy Hour, or go on a girls' holiday, or bother to fulfil your dream of training to be a yoga instructor, if you've found The One? After all, all you need is love – or so Ringo, Paul, John and George would have you believe. However, this can be a dangerous obstacle to personal growth and over time can build into insecurity and resentment; even if you don't notice it at the time, you might start to blame your partner for the thing you never did, after years or even decades of shirking the responsibility to actively bring alonement to your partnership.

It's very easy to become dependent on a partner, and many of us have fallen into the trap of leaning a little too much on someone we love. That's why, together with making time for your hobbies and social lives, it's also important to factor in some degree of emotional self-reliance, too. Camilla Thurlow acknowledged this on the podcast, when she spoke about making sure she didn't rely too much on her partner (whom she met on *Love Island*) to help her overcome social anxiety. 'I don't want to build that dynamic into my relationship,' she said. 'It's so nice to have people who support you but I want to be able to rely on myself to decompress and stop myself going through the cycles of fear.'

Relationships – of all kinds, not just romantic ones – can prove transformational in helping us evolve and grow, but, ultimately, we are alone and acknowledging that can be the saviour, rather than the ruin, of our success as a couple. That's not to say there aren't examples of lasting couples who *are* co-dependent – spending almost all of their time together, merging into an 'us' instead of an 'I' – and it seems to work for them. It can be a successful relationship model for some, but it's certainly not one that works for me or (I suspect, if you're reading this book) you. 'Clients tell me that they feel they've lost themselves and become invisible in their relationship,' Kenny adds. 'Often, they will say: "I never even noticed myself disappearing."' I don't know about you, but I find that truly heartbreaking.

'I need space'

We know that love isn't a Richard Curtis film, and yet we insist on fetishising togetherness. The newlyweds who haven't spent a day apart since they met? Your friend's parents who have been falling asleep holding hands for the past three decades? Barry and Jayne down the road who finish each other's sentences? Romantic – sure. Sustainable – for some. Don't get me wrong, I'm still a sucker for the idea of two people who can't live without each other. It's such a common trope at the end of every romantic comedy: the-mad-dash-to-the-airport-to-stop-The-One-getting-away, at the expense of their journey, not to mention a non-refundable economy plane ticket (doesn't anyone else get stressed about this?). These films revolve around a life-changing Big Love that disrupts other plans in order to serve the almighty romance gods.

It's very easy to buy into love for love's sake – and, believe me, as a fan of Richard Curtis movies, *First Dates* and Dolly Parton's greatest hits, I do it as much as the next person. It seems we can't help it; watching emotional films and TV stimulates the release of oxytocin, the 'cuddle' hormone,* effectively transforming us into human balls of goo (not the scientific term). That said, as sweet as it is to watch a couple finishing each other's sentences on television, have you ever tried having a conversation with a couple who's like that? Because it's really, really annoying.

What's also annoying is when we feel societal pressure to be with our partner at all times. Matt, 29, tells me this issue has regularly come up within his friendship group, who are almost all coupled up. 'I had plans to see a friend in the diary for a few weeks. He's usually very busy, and

---

* Paul J. Zak, 'Why Inspiring Stories Make Us React: The Neuroscience of Narrative', *Cerebrum*, 2 February 2015. https://www.ncbi.nlm.nih.gov/pmc/articles/PMC4445577

I just wanted to catch up with him one on one. But when we spoke days beforehand to confirm, it turned out he had automatically assumed we were doing something as a four with our respective girlfriends.' He suffers from the same bias when going to parties without his partner. 'I went to my friend's birthday at his house and everyone was asking where she was. She hadn't even been explicitly invited; it was just assumed we would come as a pair.'

The notion of spending time apart goes against everything we have come to expect from relationships: the romantic ideal of two people who can't be without each other; of finding your 'other half', the person who 'completes you'. But alonement has allowed me to appreciate a whole other type of togetherness – one where you mutually respect the need for time apart. This is something John Robins spoke about on the podcast. 'My partner and I support each other in whatever we want to do, so when we come together there's just so much to talk about and we really value that time.'

This rings true for Carleen, 32, who has been with her partner for eight years. 'We know that what makes us so strong as a couple is that we like doing our own thing at times and we don't resent the other person for that. We've always been able to have alone time. From the very beginning we both made it clear it was something we found important to the relationship.'

This all makes total sense, and yet the words 'I need some space' strike fear in many a loved-up heart. It can be seen as an affront, but setting a foundation of alonement within your relationship – or introducing it into an existing relationship – can vastly improve it.

Seth, 46, believes alone time is the secret to his 15-year-long marriage. He says: 'Telling someone, "I love you to the moon and back. Now please, for the love of all that is holy and good, leave me alone," is tough to say and tough to hear, but magic if you can get it right.' While Seth always needed alone time, he had never quite acknowledged it until his wife did – and previously it had been a thorn in his side: 'Up to that point I'd never really been aware of it, even though I now see my need for isolation had torpedoed a few very good relationships. I was lucky that my wife was able to see this as a component of who I am.' Yet he acknowledges the challenges, saying it took his now-wife and him a couple of years to settle into the groove of allowing each other space. 'I definitely think it is harder to get space in the beginning. It is too easy for a partner to feel insecure when you ask for space or solitude. It goes against all the romantic tropes to ask your beloved to leave you alone for a while.'

Helen, 33, shares how she negotiated this with her husband, Alex, 30, early on. 'We had a difficult conversation where we discussed the fact that the honeymoon period was wearing off and we didn't actually want to spend all of our free time together. Alex in particular felt that he was neglecting his friends and his family, and it was causing him anxiety. I felt that if I had a free evening it wasn't OK to say that I wanted to spend it on my own. It felt like a hard thing to say to each other,' admits Helen, but it has reaped rewards for them going forward, 'It took us a while, but we acknowledged that we needed to include [alone time] in our life together for our relationship to be successful.' Eight years and one wedding later, it seems to have worked.

For Jada Sezer, the ideal relationship means you're 'healthily connected but you're not co-dependent on each other. It's a partnership where you meet in the middle and support each other.' She says it took her a long time to realise that it doesn't mean somebody doesn't like you just because they have a life outside of the relationship, and rather than suffocate the other person, letting them 'have their life allows them to come back and breathe more enjoyment into the relationship'.

John Robins agrees; he advocates moving away from a 'co-dependent dynamic', because it can lead to problems further down the line: 'You get into a situation where you're always interpreting everything your partner says or does as a reflection on you and how they feel about you so if they just want some space you think, What have I done wrong?' He believes it's important to acknowledge that, if your partner needs space, 'It isn't a reflection on you [or] how they feel about you. It's quite natural for someone to need some time on their own, and I love my girlfriend just as much when I'm on my own as when I'm with her.'

In some relationships, this 'space' comes naturally, but

for others, setting the groundwork might be more challenging. Approaching your relationship through the lens of alonement will help you to have these important conversations in the most friction-less way possible. It will also help you fight the stigma around being alone that affects couples as well as single people – *where's your other half tonight? when is she moving in? do you want me to move so you can sit next to your husband?* (can you ever politely say no?) – and harness the power of alonement to reassert your independence.

Start looking for your soul, mate

While writing this chapter, I stayed in a cottage in Buckinghamshire which I rented from retired couple Catriona, 78, and Rob, 82, who live in a larger house on the same property. Catriona and Rob met when they were studying at Bristol when they were 20 and 24 respectively. They married two years later and went on to have two children. When I asked Catriona whether she had much alone time during that period, it seemed there wasn't much. 'I was a mother, a wife and a primary school teacher. There wasn't time for anything else,' she said, shrugging. Maybe this was partly to do with the *age* people used to get married. While Catriona and Rob got married relatively young by modern-day standards, in 1964, the year they married, the UK average marital age for a woman was 23 and 25 for a man.* At 22 and 26, Catriona and Rob were each only a year off the national average. For their generation, marriage was a no-brainer. 'Getting married was just what you did,' says Catriona. 'No one wanted to be left on the shelf.' Nowadays, the contemporary wisdom is that your early twenties – at the very least – are a time to explore your independence before getting 'tied down', but for women of Catriona's generation, getting married represented its own kind of freedom. 'It was a chance to get out and leave your parents' house and start a family of your own.'

Modern relationships look very different nowadays to when Catriona and Rob got together. If I think back to myself aged 20, I was living in halls at the University of Leeds and enjoying a short-lived fling with a 6'4" marijuana-smoking exchange student, known to me and my friends as, simply and accurately, 'Hot Canadian'. Hot Canadian was hardly marriage material, but in my mind he didn't need to be. The average age for the first marriage of heterosexual couples is now 31.5 and 33.4, for women and men respectively. Same-sex marriage was legalised in the UK in 2014, and the average first marriage age is even higher: 35.4 and 39.5 for lesbian and gay couples respectively.†

---

* 'Average age at first marriage, UK', *theatlas.com*, 2019. https://theatlas.com/charts/SJBFuvnc4

† Office for National Statistics, 'Marriages in England and Wales: 2016'. https://www.ons.gov.uk/peoplepopulationandcommunity/birthsdeathsandmarriages/marriagecohabitationandcivilpartnerships/bulletins/marriagesinenglandandwalesprovisional/2016

Compared with Catriona and Rob, the average young adult now has seven-odd extra years to play with before getting married. You can have sex out of wedlock (90 per cent of young couples now live together before marriage).* You can date wildly inappropriate people. You can opt out of the whole thing and give marriage a miss. Also – crucially – you can work on yourself. We live in an era of personal fulfilment, and it's widely accepted in modern culture that your twenties are an acceptable time for 'figuring things out'. Adolescence is now understood to last until you are 24, and long beyond this time you might be continuing your education, building your career and establishing yourself as an independent adult before you commit to a lifelong partnership and the conventional conveyor belt of heteronormative milestones.†
Historically, these things typically happened within the confines of marriage, particularly for women, who often lived in their parents' houses until they were married.

We are no longer rushing to get 'off the shelf' (in the absence of a suitable marital cupboard), because we have more options available to us, with or without significant others. As gender roles shift and change, it's no longer a case of slotting into a wife/mother/caregiver and husband/father/

---

* Nick Stripe, 'Married by 30? You're now in the minority', *Office for National Statistics*, blog, 1 April 2019. https://blog.ons.gov.uk/2019/04/01/married-by-30-youre-now-in-the-minority
† Katie Silver, 'Adolescence now lasts from 10 to 24', *BBC News*, 19 January 2018. https://www.bbc.co.uk/news/health-42732442

breadwinner set-up. We want to be self-actualised individuals, in our own right.

Standing – not falling – in love

Introducing alonement can help to make your relationship expectations more realistic. You call off the search for the superhero figure and concentrate on being your own saviour, relationship or otherwise. I'm reminded of when I interviewed Jane Fonda for *healthy* magazine back in 2016 (and yes, it was the highlight of my journalistic career), who told me: 'There's a reason they call it *falling* in love.' She spoke about the importance of entering a relationship standing on your own two feet – as a self-reliant individual – and then showing your partner that authentic, whole self, rather than giving up the parts of yourself that you believe seem less loveable.

As romantic as the concept of falling head over heels in love with someone is, I've come to agree. Once you value a relationship with yourself, it becomes immeasurably harder to 'fall'. Having discovered alonement, it's almost impossible to practise it without making it a value within your relationship, too. If you consider yourself whole in the first place, romantic analogies to do with 'completing' one another no longer seem so, well, romantic (call me cynical, but these days I fantasise more about having someone to help me unload the dishwasher). As the rush of new love fades away in the broad daylight of reality, it leaves behind the real question: how can you support one another to be the best version of your own unique selves? In one word: alonement.

In his book *The Art of Loving*, Erich Fromm – much like Jane Fonda – proposes a model of love which requires 'standing in love' rather than 'falling in love'. Fundamental to his relationship model is an acknowledgement of your beloved's autonomy and individuality – and a sincere desire to see that person continue to 'grow and unfold as he [or she] is'. *The Art of Loving* – somewhat ahead of its time, considering its publication in 1956 – became a global bestseller and gave Fromm a cult status. It can't have done book sales any harm that Fromm himself was in the midst of a great love of his own during the writing process, having recently married his third wife, Annis Freeman.* Erich Fromm and Annis Freeman's life together in Mexico City was characterised by alonement. Fromm would rise early, while Freeman would lie in. Fromm was immersed in building the couple's future house in Cuernavaca, a neighbouring city, while he cultivated an interest in Hasidic music and daily meditation. He was also, of course, writing his book. Freeman, meanwhile, was busy doing her thing, learning about astrology and practising tai chi. Love, according to Fromm, requires a pragmatic – and romantic – approach. His ideology offers

---

* Lawrence J. Friedman, *The Lives of Erich Fromm: Love's Prophet*.

a framework for couples to be alone, together; an example which clearly worked, if Fromm's own relationship – and the immense popularity of the book – is anything to go by.

Once you stop looking for someone to complete you, you can focus on finding someone to complement you instead. It might even change what you want from a partner – choosing someone who values their alone time too, for instance, rather than someone who wants to be together 24/7 – or allow you to value qualities in your existing partner that you never had before, like the fact that they make time for their friends. Amelia, 27, says she has actively improved her relationship with her partner, Sol, 38, through introducing more alonement: 'I feel calmer both when I'm alone and when we're together. I feel more whole and complete. The relationship, too, feels richer for it. I feel happier, which obviously means he's happier, and that we're happier together. We no longer "need" one another, which leaves space for us to "want" one another. It's overall a much more satisfying experience of being together.'

It might seem like having your cake and eating it, but the best relationships are the ones that allow for personal growth as an individual alongside your commitment to one another. When I asked my Twitter followers what made a relationship a successful one, they said:

'One where both parties can communicate their needs and feels like they are in a partnership.' Liana, 28

'Two people complementing each other's lives or creating a new one where they can both thrive.' Tom, 33

'One based on mutual respect and support. Taking the time to learn how that person needs/wants to be loved. A genuine friendship at its core, when all the cute stuff is stripped away.' Melissa, 29

'Both being happy on your own, so you're two wholes together, instead of having someone complete you.' Amy, 28

'Two wholes, not two halves.' Anna, 28

Will you be my everything?

In 2014, Eli Finkel, author and professor of psychology at Northwestern University, together with three colleagues conducted a research project which looked at modern-day American marriages. They discovered a notable shift in marital expectations; while, in the past, successful marriages were characterised by traditional gender roles and companionship, nowadays modern married couples expect to meet one another's self-expression goals (i.e. to support each other's pursuit of authenticity and personal growth). In other words, we've moved the goalposts: the traditional marital expectations of regular 'I love yous', a steady salary and a meat 'n' two veg dinner every evening are no longer enough for modern couples. We want someone who helps us become our best selves, too. Does this mean we put a tremendous amount of pressure on would-be partners to meet requirements that simply wouldn't have crossed the minds of previous generations – our grandparents, for instance? Undoubtedly. Sometimes, this can backfire and we seek an impossible Venn diagram of qualities from our other halves; piling an (arguably unrealistic) amount of expectations on to our partners to not only be a spouse or co-parent, but also a best friend, soulmate and life guru.

Whereas once upon a time marriage was based on a breadwinner/homemaker dynamic, the demands have evolved over the decades into a model of love and companionship and, in recent generations, one that also involves self-discovery and personal growth.* Increasingly, we seek a partnership that is 'heavily oriented toward esteem and self-actualisation needs'. Finkel's study found that, as spouses' marital expectations have evolved, the average modern American marriage

---

* Eli J. Finkel et al., 'The Suffocation of Marriage: Climbing Mount Maslow Without Enough Oxygen', *Psychological Inquiry* (2014), 25: 1–41. https://faculty.wcas.northwestern.edu/eli-finkel/documents/2014_FinkelHuiCarswellLarson_PsychInquiry-Copy.pdf

is significantly less happy than in previous eras, with divorce firmly on the rise, and marital satisfaction declining among those couples who stay together. Similar patterns emerge in the UK; and while, optimistically, divorce rates have fallen in recent years (currently the lowest they've been since 1971) it's also worth noting that there has been a steep decline in people getting married in the first place. That said, the best marriages are now better than ever before: Finkel and colleagues found that the happiest present-day relationships (i.e. those at the 'most satisfied' end of the spectrum, which allow for the modern goals of self-expression) are stronger than the happiest marriages of yesteryear. Our higher aspirations for marriage have proved something of a double-edged sword, but, last time I checked, we're not going backwards. A phenomenon called the 'Michelangelo Effect' – named after Michelangelo's ability to chisel blocks of marble into perfection – seems to justify our sky-high ambitions for our relationships: psychologists have found that we are more likely to develop into the person we want to be if we have a close romantic partner who supports our goals.*

It's a hard balance to get right, and it's worth remembering you have many other relationships in your life, like friends, family and colleagues, as well as your partner; you simply can't rely on one person (other than yourself) to meet all your

---

* Caryl E. Rusbult et al., 'The Michelangelo Phenomenon', *Current Directions in Psychological Science* (2009), 18 (6). https://faculty.wcas.northwestern.edu/eli-finkel/documents/47_RusbultFinkelKumashiro2009_CDir.pdf

needs. But here's what I propose for an alonement-inspired modern relationship: what if you place value in a partner who you love being around, but who can also comfortably allow you the space to pursue your passions and ambitions, while they do the same? A partner who constantly inspires you with their own endeavours, offering support when you need it but allowing you to fly? Who takes pleasure in your happiness and success, and vice versa? Idealistic, perhaps; but it's certainly no more so than the notion that one person can give you everything, so it's undoubtedly something to strive for.

'They were living separate lives'

Is there such a thing as too much time apart? In other words, how long before you're leading 'separate lives' – a phrase that tends to be thrown out like an epitaph about a failed relationship? 'That's not something you can set a rule around,' offers dating expert Hayley Quinn, in an interview for this chapter. 'You just have to have a compatible understanding of what that is.' Quinn cites a couple she knows who have been together for five years. During that time, one of them lived in Japan for a year, but since they've moved in together they have kept separate bedrooms. This set-up works for them. Julie Telvi, a family and couple psychotherapist, argues that every relationship needs to create its own 'couple culture' around what feels right and comfortable, through a process of 'negotiation and compromise'. She says: 'It is important for the couple to have a shared understanding about what amount of alone time they need to address their individual needs and what amount of time they need qualitatively or quantitatively to nurture their relationship.'

The 'right' balance can change over time, too. Telvi, who has been married for 33 years, regards alone time as 'a commodity which fluctuates depending on supply and demand'. She says of her own relationship: 'My husband and I went through many different life stages together and those periods somewhat dictated how much time we spent alone. For example, when the children were very little and dependent on us, we actively tried to give space and alone time to the other. As we got older and the children flew the nest, there were more opportunities to spend time alone – so it started to feel less valuable. So, we spent time thinking about finding activities to do together.'

Hilary, 55, and her husband Sandro, 70, have a particularly unique 'couple culture' – to use Telvi's phrase. They have been together since they met in 1997, when she was a student and he a teacher on a wine course in Florence, Italy, and married in 2014. All this time, they have lived in separate countries: her in the UK, he still in Florence. She says: 'We never made a conscious decision at the start to stay together but apart; it just happened. As time has gone on, we have remained aware that each of us likes what we do and where we do it, nor do we have jobs which translate well to the other's country. He is a foodie, a sommelier and a Master of Food, with his specialism being olive oil. He also works as a food journalist and for the campaigning organisation Slow Food. I could teach English in Italy but in a high school, I would earn about a third of what I do here. The alternative would be business English, which would be my idea of hell.'

While Hilary and Sandro's set-up might not be for everyone, Hilary mentions it certainly inspires envy in some of her friends – 'particularly the female ones' – to whom being married, but not 'married' seems ideal. She adds: 'One of the men who proposed a toast at our wedding commented on the fact that many people choose to live together without being married but we were the only couple he knew who chose to marry but not live together.'

While some might perceive the notion of 'leading separate lives' as a warning sign of a doomed relationship, Emma Kenny regards it as crucial, not just for the success of your relationship but for the success of your life within it. This is not, by any means, a suggestion that you shouldn't pursue quality time with your partner; it's just to say you should also remain attuned to your own autonomy and individual goals alongside that.

Of course, when you're in a loving relationship, it's not just about suiting your own needs – it's about getting a healthy balance that works for you both. If someone is by nature emotionally reticent or dismissive of your quality time needs, then it's absolutely within your rights to communicate what you want and to ask for them to meet you halfway. It's a balancing act. Equally, if you've started introducing more alonement in your life, it's imperative that you communicate that to your partner so they know you're not avoiding them, or having a hot affair with your PT. Lending them this book could be a good start. It might even be a force for connection, suggests Kenny: 'Encourage your partner to have their own space to do their own thing . . . then show an interest in that aloneness.' Quinn agrees with this approach. 'You can't get all your needs met through one person. You can encourage someone to spend time with friends or family to meet their needs through multiple sources, not just through the relationship.'

Amelia did this with her boyfriend and soon felt the benefits: 'I have been encouraging Sol to have more time alone: with his friends outside the relationship, engaging in solo hobbies and exercising alone. Although I haven't told him about alonement; I've just been making gentle suggestions here and there and he's definitely benefiting. I can see it in him, and he has said to me that he feels better.'

So, as ever, it's about good communication. But what can you do if alonement is proving a hard sell to your partner?

Opposites attract

Acknowledging the need for alonement can be particularly important when one half of the couple feels a greater need for alone time than the other. In Chapter 1, I discuss the difference between introverted and extroverted types, and the different 'energy' needs. While time alone can be energising for the former, it can seem less valuable for the latter, which can cause a problem in relationships (not unlike a mismatched libido). As Quinn says: 'Acceptance is more important than understanding. You may not fully relate to someone's reasons but it's being able to accept a person how they are and with what they're able to offer. With that acceptance you can enjoy a relationship; when you manoeuvre it can cause conflict.'

Nanotechnologist and science educator Michelle Dickinson shared with me on the podcast that she identifies as an introvert, whereas her husband is an extreme extrovert. She admitted that it had been hard at the beginning of their relationship to accept each other's differences, but clear communication and mutual understanding over time has helped them to respect each other's social needs. She now feels perfectly content to leave a party early, without it causing a scene, and leaving her husband to party on into the small hours. She even created an alter ego, Nanogirl, to help her feel more confident in social situations.

Helen, who also identifies as more of an introvert, explains how she manages this with her husband, Alex. 'I've always been a person who needs time on my own. I was a child who'd happily spend hours playing by myself and my need to be on my own has continued into adulthood so it's very important to the success of our relationship that I'm able to do that.' So, what happens when Helen doesn't get alone time? 'It's a disaster! I really struggle without time to myself and start to retreat inwards just to feel like I have some mental space. We have boring conversations that annoy us both, we snap at each other and we become less intimate. There's very little motivation to be affectionate with a person who you've been having bad-tempered conversations with all day.'

For new couples

As a new couple, factoring alone time into your budding romance can feel about as natural as a handbrake turn, particularly if you're convinced you've finally found The One after years of searching. There's also a risk that advocating for alone time may cause unwanted tension or hurt feelings during the mushy early stages of a relationship, which are notoriously a minefield of unintended slights and potential misunderstandings because you don't actually know each other all that well. For instance, it's hard not to take it the wrong way when someone you're dating leaves your place at

7am the morning after to go to the gym, rather than staying for coffee and bagels (yet you become infinitely more reassured once you learn you're dating an early-rising, HIIT-obsessed intermittent faster).

It's a tricky balance to get right, and it might be tempting for you (and whoever you're dating) to de-prioritise time alone at this stage of a relationship – but, according to Quinn, you should be starting as you mean to carry on, and establishing healthy boundaries. She says: 'Avoid the temptation to drop all the things that kept you sane and stable pre the relationship. It's very tempting when you meet someone you like to clear your diary out, but it's important to preserve that space to yourself and give yourself clarity about how you think and feel in the relationship.' Jada Sezer agrees with this philosophy, suggesting on the podcast that the first year of your relationship is an important time to establish your boundaries, even if this requires 'awkward conversations at the very start'.

How do you prevent your new partner from taking this the wrong way? Communication is key. 'At the start of a relationship you don't have a depth of knowledge about someone to understand why they're doing things, so it's easy to misinterpret someone not wanting to see you,' says Quinn. 'Express that [alone time] is one of your values. Say that having a couple of evenings a week watching box sets by yourself is an important space. If you give that person that piece of information, then you give them the opportunity to understand.'

Establishing regular things you like to do alone, and letting your partner know about them early on, is crucial. A helpful way to initiate a conversation with your partner might start with you asking about their *own* need for time alone (they may surprise you!). This allows alonement to be understood as a regular, recalibrating time, rather than a crisis or a sign anything's wrong with your relationship. As for the phrasing? You might call this time apart your alonement or 'free time'. Amelia has dubbed her alonement 'Amelia Time'. 'That way it's about me and not about [my boyfriend], which "I need to be alone", might imply.'

For established couples

You might be reading this and thinking, OK, but what if I've been with someone long term and we still haven't nailed the whole alonement thing? Introducing alonement when you've been together a while is a different kettle of fish. By this point, you will be a team, and it's more about incorporating it into your life together as a shared value. We all know that relationships change and adapt in order to thrive, so it might help to approach alonement as a way to make your relationship stronger, rather than as a sign of weakness.

This all starts with simply talking about alonement and why you think it's important (again, handing over this book might save your breath). But habits don't change overnight, particularly if you've settled into a routine and feel bogged down by what you've 'always done' as a couple. This can often come down to a loss of confidence in your ability to do things alone, which Kenny says is common in long-term relationships: 'When this happens, you get stuck in your ways because it's what you know.'

Kenny recommends a process of discovering alonement opportunities in your day-to-day life, through journalling. Spend five minutes writing down three things you might enjoy doing alone, and one thing you struggle to do alone (which you might treat as a challenge). This might be as simple as going for a coffee or taking a day trip somewhere. Encourage your partner to make their own list, so you're in it together. Beyond this, Kenny recommends exposure to help you regain your confidence: 'Go for coffee by yourself. Put yourself out there – and know you don't have to enjoy it the first time around.'

Start looking for role models outside your relationship and immediate circle to help inspire your newfound independence, recommends Kenny. This is unlikely to be a couple – more likely an individual with their own strong sense of identity. Ask yourself, *Who are those people – and why do they inspire passion in me?* Maybe it's Charlotte at work, who did a charity bungee jump. Think about what you could do that might be equally vital and interesting – and how you might bring that into your life.

Finally, sometimes it takes doing bold things to create a shift in your relationship dynamic, like booking a hiking holiday in Portugal that you've always wanted to go on. Essentially, whether or not alonement has been a value in your relationship before, it's something you can introduce at any time. Remember the couple, Catriona and Rob, who I mentioned earlier in this chapter? At the age of 70, Catriona invested in a cottage on the Isle of Lewis in the Outer Hebrides – her favourite place in the world. She visits alone, several times a year, for week-long periods, while her husband goes walking in Exmoor National Park in the southwest of England. 'We go off and do our own thing,' she tells me, eyes sparkling. 'Then we come together again and talk about it.' As Catriona will testify – it's never too late.

Relationship status: Alonement

For most of my life, finding love was a priority, but I was looking for it for all the wrong reasons. Primarily, it was to bring an ultimate meaning to my life; to activate my Happily Ever After. Perhaps this is the result of growing up on a diet of romantic comedies, love songs and happily married parents. But, deep down, I think I was also trying to escape the inconvenient fact that, relationship or not, I will always be alone, with the mammoth task of making my own hopes and dreams come true, All By Myself. It's taken me two years, but I'm now on board with that essential aloneness. Dare I say, I'm eternally committed to retaining it. My quest for love looks radically different now that I'm looking for a partner I can stand beside, thinking: 'I don't need you, but I want you in my life.'

As for navigating that aloneness within a serious relationship – that's still to come. Suffice to say, I never managed it personally in the past, and I've got to hand it to all the couples I've spoken to as I researched this book: they're doing a brilliant job. As a single person, you're regularly quizzed about your dating life, and it's rare you get to turn the tables and ask lots of nosy questions about people's relationships, as I did for this book. Through my very important investigation, I've discovered that bringing alonement into your relationship often isn't easy, but it's worth it. When it works, it's aspirational, and should honestly get as much air-time as date nights.

While I've spent the past two years single, alonement has allowed me to bring so much more to my relationships with my family and friends, so I can only hope and trust this will translate into a romantic relationship too. I'm optimistic for the future. Maybe I'll never fall in love, but that's OK – I'd rather stand, side by side. That way I'll never lose myself again.

ALONE FOREVER?

Alonement started as a New Year's resolution, but it snow-balled into something much bigger, expanding over the past two years into a podcast, a newsletter, a trademark, a whole community of people and – now – this very book.

Time alone was once my biggest fear – and, in this, I learnt that I was not alone. Avoiding being alone is both a primal instinct – a fear of being away from the pack – and, increasingly, a modern anxiety. In a noisy, ever-distracted world, we've normalised the inability to be safe in our own minds to the point that even the most confident among us still fear being alone in all its guises: single, away from your partner or housemates, without your phone, working from home. The only solution for this fear is to confront it, but first you have to believe in what's on the other side.

I first made that New Year's resolution because I didn't

want a fear of being alone to define my life, and I've written this book because I don't want it to define yours, either. Life is too short, precious and full of opportunities to be dictated by fear; least of all a fear of yourself. I want you to know that it may be hard, but it will never not be worth it. Time getting to know yourself is the best and most empowering investment you can ever make, and in doing so you will make yourself a partner for life.

Alonement allows you to be in the driving seat of your own life. It's how you learn to form healthy relationships with others and build a positive relationship with yourself.* Time alone is not time wasted; it's the chance to harness your own, unique power and tap into your inner sense of wonder. I'm not pretending we don't live in a society where being alone can prove difficult to navigate, at least in certain situations. Attending a wedding solo, paying a single supplement for a hotel room or, as I experienced, being thrown out of a café because you're quietly reading in a corner challenges our right to be alone. And yet, what if the system is broken, not us? That's why we have to normalise aloneness, so it will become easier for everyone. Plus, once you've recognised the benefits of alonement, these obstacles will seem much less significant.

Of course, while I've brought in the important stories of

---

* Reed W. Larson, 'The Emergence of Solitude as a Constructive Domain of Experience in Early Adolescence', *Child Development*, 68 (1): 80–93. https://srcd. onlinelibrary.wiley.com/doi/abs/10.1111/j.1467-8624.1997.tb01927.x

others to write this book, it is inspired first and foremost by my own experience. When I made that New Year's resolution, I never could have imagined how much it would change my life. After years of outsourcing my hopes, dreams and innermost emotions to others, I've finally come back to myself. I feel whole, and never lacking. *Alonement has made me feel normal for wanting time away from my partner*, a podcast listener told me recently. For many others, it's normalised the everyday bursts of aloneness that we never quite knew how to talk about. A little space for yourself in a busy world; simply a pocket of time away to breathe. A moment of calm, to hear yourself and recalibrate.

Until now we've lacked the vocabulary to communicate this essential need to ourselves and others. To describe being alone as something of value, rather than a stick to beat ourselves with, or a concerning habit of withdrawal. And that's why alonement isn't just a trendy word; it embodies what I hope will be a cultural shift. It's the language we need to begin to cherish, communicate and capitalise on that primal feeling of aloneness with ourselves, in order to recognise it as the goddamned superpower that it is. As for that dirty word, loneliness? I can't promise that learning to value alonement will always protect you from being lonely – we all have our good and bad days. I still get lonely sometimes, too, but I'm able to recognise that feeling for what it is – a natural desire to be around my nearest and dearest – rather than confuse it with a desperate bid to get away from myself at any cost.

Once you've learnt to find joy in time spent alone, loneliness is much less likely to rear its ugly head. And when it does? Alone doesn't have to mean lonely, but sometimes it does and that's OK; what's important is that you know there's an alternative.

After two years of writing about being alone, I've never felt so socially connected – not just to my loved ones but also to the wider alonement community. To paraphrase bell hooks, once you value your own company, other people are more than just a way to escape; to still your thoughts; to facilitate your adventures. Your relationships become stronger, calmer, less weighed down with unrealistic expectations. You still rely on people, but for the right reasons: because they feed your soul; because you respect them as individuals; because you love their company; because they offer a fresh perspective on the world. And, although you can never presume to know them as well as you know yourself, you will always try, reaching out your soul to theirs, each alone yet connected in mutual aloneness.

I know that nothing is out of bounds as long as I'm brave enough to go at it alone. I'm excited to spend a lifetime with myself, and excited about who I might meet along the way. Alone doesn't scare me anymore. And nor should it scare you. Because you, alone, are enough.

GLOSSARY

Alonement
Celebrating and valuing the time you spend alone as positive, joyful and/or regenerative.

Amatonormativity
As coined by Arizona State University professor of philosophy Elizabeth Brake in 2016, 'the assumption that a central, exclusive, amorous relationship is normal for humans, in that it is a universally shared goal, and that such a relationship is normative'.

Compromise-by-default
When you compromise your needs or desires out of habit, without even knowing you're doing it.

Eudaimonic
Of happiness, associated with finding long-term meaning and purpose.

Hedonic
Of happiness, associated with short-term pleasure and enjoyment.

Ikigai
A Japanese concept that means 'a reason for being', sometimes translated as the thing that gets you out of bed in the morning.

Intrinsic motivation
When you are driven by internal forces to do something, rather than external motivation.

Mindfulness
The state of focusing your consciousness on one thing at a time.

Only Me-ism
When you deny yourself comfort or effort, out of a belief that you're less important because you're by yourself.

Positive selfishness
Looking out for your own needs in a way that helps you be a better person to others, and isn't to the detriment of anyone else.

Rubbernecking

When you fixate on someone else's life, often via social media, rather than focusing on your own.

Saturday Scaries

Anxiety centring around not having anything to do on a Saturday night.

Self-actualisation

Fulfilling your individual potential.

Self-care

Any activity we do deliberately in order to protect our mental, emotional and physical health.

Single positivity

A movement centred around celebrating singledom as a positive, fulfilling experience.

Single supplement

A travel industry premium charged to solo guests occupying one room by themselves.

Solitude skills

Personal skills centred around spending time alone, and doing it well (as opposed to social skills).

RECOMMENDED READING

Aziz Ansari, *Modern Romance* (2015)

Poorna Bell, *In Search of Silence* (2019)

Bella DePaulo, *Alone: The Badass Psychology of People Who Like Being Alone* (2017)

Chidera Eggerue, *What A Time To Be Alone* (2018)

Erich Fromm, *The Art of Loving* (1956)

Elizabeth Gilbert, *Big Magic* (2015)

Florence Given, *Women Don't Owe You Pretty* (2020)

Catherine Grey, *The Unexpected Joy of Being Single* (2019)

Michael Harris, *Solitude: In Pursuit of a Singular Life in a Crowded World* (2017)

Marjorie Hillis, *Live Alone and Like It* (1936)

Sara Maitland, *How To Be Alone* (2014)

Stephanie Rosenbloom, *Alone Time* (2019)

The School of Life, *An Emotional Education* (2019)

The School of Life, *A Replacement for Religion* (2020)

Virginia Woolf, *A Room of One's Own* (1929)

ACKNOWLEDGEMENTS

I wrote this book alone, but never in isolation. As the following list will testify, **it truly takes a village**. Alonement started as something I dared to dream up in my yellow diary, yet it's only because of the generous support and blind faith of others that it now exists as an actual, real-life book (also with a joy-giving, bright-yellow cover).

Zoe Abrahams and Rachel Tan – you know this book would never have happened without the pair of you. I may have come up with alonement by myself, but you breathed the necessary life and hope into this idea in its infancy, when we stayed up talking until midnight on that dark, rainy Monday night that seems so long ago now. From our dedicated 'alonement' WhatsApp group to Rachel's design skills and Zoe's can-do consultancy to make crazy ideas actually happen, you've so generously shared your genius brains and also your hearts – and for that I'm forever grateful. You've been constants at my side throughout, plotting, laughing and celebrating at every step of the way, a trail of A3 sketch pads and champagne corks in our wake. *We did it.*

Nor would this have been possible without the support of my family: thank you Beverley and Ken, aka Mum and Dad – best friends and irreverent comedy-duo as well as parents – for your boundless love, kindness and encouragement throughout not just the past few months of writing, but my whole life. Mum, for being my first trusted editor (your eagle-eyed talent amazes me), and Dad for showing me it's possible to make big dreams come true. Thank you to my brother, Andrew, for always inspiring and helping me and never failing to offer an intelligent new perspective. Being able to share this with you all has meant the world.

I owe the hugest thank yous to Alison MacDonald – my editor and guardian angel at Quercus, for believing in this book from the start and tirelessly working to bring it into existence, ever since that first coffee meeting on Valentine's Day (*it was fate!*) – and my incredible agent, Rowan Lawton, for her stellar advice, support and humour at every stage of the way. Together, you are the dream team. Thank you also to the wider team at Quercus, including Bethan Ferguson, Katya Ellis, Lipfon Tang, Hannah Cawse and Hannah Winter.

Next, the Friends of My Dreams – who have shown their unwavering support over the writing period, and have each contributed to this book's contents. Thank you, Liana Telvi; Hannah Epstein; Hayley Lewis; my Sassy Babes – I *still* hate the name – Victoria Beardwood, Mariana Cerqueira, Lauren Clark, Anna Cafolla, Eli Court and Emily Wadsworth; Bex Shapiro; Amy Yiannitsarou and Amy Lo; Alex and Helen Fenton; Carla Smith; Tom Ough; Guy Peleg; Zahra Azam; Jodie Coller; Andri Hadjichristou; and all my former Yahoo colleagues: Clare Hindson, Jessica Morgan, Alexandra Thompson, Maisie Bovingdon, Nadia Sekabanja, Caithlin 'The Oracle' Mercer. Thank you for lighting up my life and keeping me sane, too.

I also owe a special thank you to Chris De Kauwe; Megan Daly; Frances Bibby; Tam Malley; Nicola Slawson (of the inimitable Single Supplement newsletter); Katie Rudin; Matt Keston; Jamie Willcocks; Steve Ware; Rosie Dutton; Hilary and Eli Keren; the wonderful *HuffPost* team; Rhiannon Evans at *Grazia* (for the feature commission that changed everything!). Thank you to the experts I interviewed for this book – including Julie Telvi; Emma Kenny; Suzy Reading; Hayley Quinn; Dr Virginia Thomas; Bella DePaulo; Michael Harris; Sally Baker; and to everyone who so generously agreed to be a case study. There are too many of you to thank individually, but know I am so grateful to all of you for investing in this concept and keeping me motivated, and for showing enthusiasm and encouragement along the way.

Thank you to my brilliant extended family, with a special shout-out to Viv, Henry and Sam Churney and Natalie and Craig Fox, who have always encouraged my writing (from the tender age of four!), and my grandparents Jean and Charlie, who inspired a chapter in this book. I'm so grateful to have you all.

This book is made immeasurably richer thanks to the contributions of my podcast guests from seasons 1 and 2; thank you to Daisy Buchanan, Alain de Botton, Jo Good, Vick Hope, Camilla Thurlow, Matthew Stadlen, Poorna Bell, Alice Liveing, Alexandra Shulman, Jada Sezer, Derek Owusu, Felicity Cloake, Konnie Huq, Eric Klinenberg, Dr Michelle Dickinson, Sophia Money-Coutts, John Robins, Jonny Benjamin, Florence Given, Shani Silver. I learnt so much from speaking to each and every one of you, and it has been the biggest honour to interview such a fascinating and inspirational line-up of people. Thanks also to Martin Kimber, whose podcast production knowledge, gallows humour and radical honesty helped me get this show off the ground.

Thank you to the brilliant Chamomile café in north London – where I've always been welcomed as a customer, solo or otherwise, and where I wrote the final quarter of this book at the end of lockdown. You are my spiritual home.

Finally, I am so eternally grateful to the wider alonement community, for all your kind words and messages over the past year and a half. Thank you for never letting me feel 'alone' in championing alonement and for so candidly sharing your own experiences with me. This is for you all.